Infant Baptism

and the Silence of the New Testament

Infant Baptism

and the Silence of the New Testament

Bryan Holstrom

Ambassador International
GREENVILLE, SOUTH CAROLINA & BELFAST, NORTHERN IRELAND

www.emeraldhouse.com

Infant Baptism and the Silence of the New Testament

Printed in the United States of America

ISBN 978-1-932307-70-2

Cover design & page layout by David Siglin of A&E Media

AMBASSADOR INTERNATIONAL
Emerald House
427 Wade Hampton Blvd.
Greenville, SC 29609, USA
www.emeraldhouse.com

AMBASSADOR PUBLICATIONS
Providence House
Ardenlee Street
Belfast, BT6 8QJ
Northern Ireland, UK
www.ambassador-productions.com

The colophon is a trademark of Ambassador

To Meredith

"O my love, you are as beautiful as Tirzah, lovely as Jerusalem, awesome as an army with banners!"
S<small>ONG OF</small> S<small>OLOMON</small> 6:4

Table of Contents

Foreword

In 1 Corinthians 12:13, Paul tells the church that "in one Spirit" Christians have been "baptized into one body." Baptism is a rich and complex sign that symbolizes union with Christ, regeneration, and the forgiveness of sins, and Paul here points to another aspect of baptism. Baptism is a sign of unity of the Christian church. Through much of church history baptism has indeed served that function. Despite the many divisions and rivalries among Christians, they share a common bond of being baptized into the name of the Father, Son, and Holy Spirit.

Since the time of the Reformation, however, baptism ironically has also served as a source of disunity for the church. Protestants and Roman Catholics, in the midst of their broader disagreements about salvation, disagreed about the effects of baptism. Yet most Protestants and Roman Catholics continued to agree at least about who should be baptized: converts to Christianity and the children of believers. The early dissenters from this consensus— the Anabaptists—were opposed by Protestants and Catholics alike, not only for their doctrine of baptism but also for their radical views on many other theological and social issues. But as time moved on groups of Baptists emerged who were much less radical than the Anabaptists but shared their basic conviction that only people who make a personal profession of faith should be baptized. Some of these Baptists even held views of salvation nearly identical to the convictions of Reformed and Presbyterian Christians, professing belief in divine sovereignty and the justification of sinners by faith alone. And thus was born one of the tragic divisions of the Christian church that endures to the present day—a division centering upon the sacrament that unites Christians as one body in Christ.

Bryan Holstrom has written his book against the background of this tragedy. His view is simple: Scripture teaches that the children of believers should be baptized and the Christian church should again unite in the practice of paedobaptism. Holstrom makes his case in exactly the right way. He is clear about where he stands and he argues his position rigorously and engagingly. He bases his claims not upon his own opinions or clever syllogisms but upon careful interpretation of Scripture. He gives no quarter to his Baptist interlocutors yet appeals to them winsomely as brothers in Christ—with a firm but gentle spirit. He presses the point that rejecting infant baptism is not a minor error, for it concerns more than just baptism but also the whole biblical story of God's redeeming work among his people. Whatever the initial attractions of a Baptist position, Holstrom points to the beauty of God's covenants with his people through history and the abundant blessing of the inclusion of children in the covenant relationship.

Many books have been written about baptism, but Holstrom adds a distinctive voice to the literature. Unlike the authors of most baptism books, Holstrom is not a trained theologian. He has done his research and writes very clearly, but his perspective is entirely that of the church, not the academy. He himself was an adult convert to the faith and was rebaptized. But after much study he embraced a paedobaptist position and now serves as an elder in a congregation of the Orthodox Presbyterian Church. His zeal for his subject arises out of his own experience, his conversations with those holding a Baptist position, and his pastoral concerns for the flock of Christ. The result is a book perfectly designed for the thoughtful Christian without formal theological education. It is a concise yet surprisingly thorough biblical case for paedobaptism that readers will not easily be able to ignore.

Holstrom does not ignore the difficult questions but takes them head on. In his own experience he has repeatedly heard an objection that many people think is conclusive: the New Testament is silent on infant baptism. Those who hold a Baptist position may be surprised to find Holstrom turning this objection on its head. The New Testament's failure to address infant baptism explicitly is not an argument against infant baptism but an argument for it. Holstrom effectively shows how the unity of God's covenantal dealings with his people through history means that if the New Testament does not repeal the principle that children of believers belong to the covenant then the New Testament evidently continues to embrace it. It is no accident that the apostles baptized whole households just as the Old Testament saints circumcised their households.

Bryan Holstrom has written an excellent book and I hope that it gets into the hands of many readers. He has served the church and the cause of biblical truth well. Those holding a Baptist view will find themselves challenged in the best sort of way—by a thorough exploration of biblical teaching. Paedobaptists themselves will be pushed to think in richer and more biblically consistent ways about their practice of infant baptism. May this book serve to heal divisions in Christ's church and to encourage Christians to embrace more meaningfully the covenant promises of God for themselves and their children.

David VanDrunen
Robert B. Strimple Professor of Systematic Theology and Christian Ethics
Westminster Seminary California

Preface

This book is born, at least partially, out of frustration – a growing frustration at what I perceive to be a near-total lack of understanding concerning the doctrine of baptism in the Christian church today. Few people are able to articulate the reasons why some churches adhere to the historic practice of baptizing their infant members. Even fewer seem willing to defend the practice. This work intends to do just that – and to do so passionately!

Of course, you would be warranted in asking what this book, amongst the hundreds available on the subject, could possibly have to offer that the others do not; for it is undeniable that there are many excellent works that have been written over the centuries and are still available for public consumption by those wanting to gain a deeper understanding of the issues surrounding Christian baptism. Nevertheless, I have approached the subject with certain perspectives and goals in mind which I pray has resulted in a work that many will find helpful.

In the first place, the present work is an attempt to offer a biblical defense of infant baptism that will be accessible to even the most theologically-untrained Christian who desires to know more about the subject. While a rudimentary knowledge of the Bible and its contents will be helpful to any reader of this book, most will be glad to know that they will need neither a theological dictionary, nor a Hebrew/Greek lexicon, at hand as they proceed through it. Although a few terms and concepts will be unfamiliar to some readers, I have attempted to define them in as simple and straightforward a manner as is possible without compromising their essential meaning. Thus, the book is intended to be relatively simple, though hopefully not simplistic.

Second, the present work is intended to be relatively short, though still interact with and address all major aspects of the debate surrounding baptism. One can easily find some excellent works on the subject which are of the church "book rack" variety, but their limited size does not allow their authors to develop the doctrine to any great extent, much less interact with, and answer, opposing views. On the other hand, there are some very good works which give a fairly comprehensive defense of infant baptism in only 200-300 pages. But even that modest length is enough to cause more than a few casual Christian readers to avoid the task altogether.

This book represents an attempt to find a happy medium between the two. For those who want or need more than a pamphlet-sized treatment, yet may not want to slog through a 300-page book, I hope this work will fill the bill. I have sought to write a book that would allow someone who was familiar with its contents to make a sixty second case for infant baptism, if necessary, and yet would provide enough grist for a more extended defense and discussion of the topic as well. Of course, that means that some arguments have received far less development than their importance to the subject would indicate, or I would have preferred, but that is the price that must be paid for achieving the balance I have sought from the outset. Readers who are interested in taking the next step to a more detailed discussion of the subject will discover plenty of helpful resources for further study by simply scanning the footnotes interspersed throughout the book.

Finally, the line of argumentation found in this book is a bit unique, since it represents an attempt to interact with the questions which I have personally heard raised by others over the years when discussing this subject. I have largely set out to follow the thread of 'silence' (i.e., the lack of an explicit command) concerning infant baptism in the New Testament, and demonstrate where it leads us in the debate over this practice. I have done so because, in my own interactions with individual Christians on this subject, this has been the most common charge leveled against infant baptism by those who hold to a believer's baptism position. If the 'silence' of the New Testament is supposedly the Achilles Heel of the doctrine of infant baptism, then any work which seeks to prove the biblical case for it must meet this objection head-on and deal with it forthrightly and completely. This work attempts to do just that.

It is important to recognize at the outset that the case for infant baptism is a cumulative one. That is, no single argument or portion of the case may be seen as sufficient to establish the validity of infant baptism on its own, but I believe that when all of the pieces are put in place and considered as a whole, the case is a strong one.

Although I trust that the passion which I have for the practice of infant baptism will be evident throughout the book, I have tried my best not to caricature or misconstrue the views of those who would take issue with my own position. Frankly, to do so would be self-defeating, since I believe that the case for infant baptism is a strong one which speaks for itself, and that the only reason that it is not embraced by more evangelical Christians today is because they have never heard the arguments for it.

Throughout the book I have used the designation 'Baptist' to describe those churches and individual Christians who hold to a believer's baptism position. This view holds that baptism is reserved for those who are of a sufficient age to express individual faith in Jesus Christ, and thus, is not to be administered to infants under any circumstances. Of course, not everyone who holds to such a position attends a church with the 'Baptist' identification in its name. In fact, the believer's baptism position is far and away the majority position in evangelical churches today, many of which have no denominational affiliation at all.

On the other hand, I have used the designation 'Reformed' to describe those churches and Christians who adhere to the practice of baptizing the infant children of church members, which was not only the practice of the churches of the Reformation in the sixteenth century, but of the early church as well.

I realize that some will object to using these terms to delineate the two sides in this debate, especially since the author is well aware that there are not a few churches and Christians who adhere to believer's baptism and also hold to the doctrines of grace which characterized the truth recovered by the churches of the Reformation. Nevertheless, for reasons which will become clear as you proceed through the book, I no longer believe that the term 'Reformed Baptist' is either a helpful or accurate one.

Moreover, at least in this case, it is a more accurate way of delineating the differences than by use of the terms Baptist and Paedobaptist, as is often done, since there are actually *several different* paedobaptist theologies of the sacrament, and this is an effort to defend only the traditional *Reformed* understanding of the meaning and purpose of baptism. Indeed, all other paedobaptist theologies of baptism are explicitly rejected.

Because I believe so strongly in the blessing and significance of baptizing covenant children, it is my hope that many who read this book will be persuaded of the biblical case for it. But if my own feeble efforts at persuasion fail to convince even one single reader, it will be enough if all who do read it will praise the name of Jesus Christ for giving us this sign and seal of His promise to deliver and care for His people. That is the real purpose for which it has been written.

Chapter 1

Introduction

1994 was a big year for me. As the year opened I graduated from Law School. A couple of months later I sat for the Bar exam, which was the final step toward the beginning of my new chosen line of work. I was thirty-five years old and had already been gainfully employed for many years in another line of work. So with a great deal of excitement, and some trepidation, I set out on an entirely new career path.

In the late summer I secured my first position as an attorney with a small suburban law firm, packed up my belongings, and moved from my apartment on the north side of Chicago to the western suburbs forty miles away to begin my new adventure.

As it turns out, my legal career was short-lived, lasting only about a year and a half. But the year of 1994 brought about far more significant and permanent changes in my spiritual life, for it was during this time that I became a Christian. Through the preaching of the Word I was converted from the useless idols that had occupied my life up until that time, and turned in faith to the living and true God (1 Thess. 1:9).

Embracing my newfound faith meant searching for a church home, where that faith would be nurtured and strengthened. In short order I found just such a church. It was a wonderful body of believers who were committed to the truth of Scripture and the doctrines of grace, the set of teachings concerning salvation that the Reformed churches had embraced in their break with Rome in the sixteenth century. Simply put, the doctrines of grace affirm the Bible's teachings that man plays no part in his own salvation, save that of receiving the gift of faith which God, out of His grace, gives to certain persons. Man, then, is not the principal actor in the great drama of salvation; he is acted upon by God. As the Reformers were fond of saying, 'Salvation is all of grace.'

My new church was committed to the Bible's teaching on this fundamental question. But it was also a Baptist church, committed to the practice of believer's baptism. At the time, however, this suited me just fine. The prospect of being able to publicly affirm my newfound faith by undergoing rebaptism (I had been baptized as an infant), coupled with the fact that as a single man I was not yet contemplating any infant baptisms in my future, made the whole matter of infant baptism somewhat unimportant to me at the time.

Anyway, less than two years out of law school, I found myself back at the books, this time studying theology. Over the next few years, I spent nearly every non-working hour studying Scripture and reading the works of the great (and not-so-great) Christian writers from the past and present, expounding upon almost every conceivable subject relating to the Christian faith and life. But I had never undertaken any systematic study of the subject of baptism.

For years now I had heard that infant baptism was a relic of the past, a holdover from the Roman Church, assumed by the Reformed churches as a matter of expediency, and resulting in what one noted author and pastor has described as an "incomplete Reformation." And I had simply bought into such a notion without any further investigation of my own. After all, it seemed to be a perfectly reasonable argument. I couldn't find any place in Scripture where parents were commanded to baptize their children, nor could I locate a single explicit reference to the rite being administered to any child of tender age in the New Testament.

Nevertheless, as I continued to read the great writers of the past, men with names such as Luther, Calvin, Zwingli, Knox, Henry, Baxter, Owen, Edwards, Dabney, Hodge, and Warfield, I couldn't help noticing that, although these men came from slightly different Reformed backgrounds (some were Presbyterian, some were Congregationalist, and a few were Anglican or Lutheran), they were all agreed on this – that the practice of infant baptism was a scriptural one.

To be fair, there were some great writers of the Baptist persuasion from those centuries as well, men such as John Gill, John Bunyan, and Charles Spurgeon. But it struck me that there were far fewer of them. Of course, there have been times in the history of the church when only the brave few were engaged in fighting for the truth of a scriptural principle against the overwhelming tide of theological opinion.

But such did not seem to be the case here, for the men who had embraced infant baptism were all beholden to the truth of Scripture, and it didn't seem fitting to attribute their belief in the practice to one of expediency. These men never determined anything on the basis of what was expedient. In many cases, they risked their very lives to stand on the principle of truth, and they were not men who were given to simply accepting received traditions of the past without requiring a full-fledged biblical basis for them. An untold numbers of traditions, including that of baptismal regeneration, were abandoned by the Reformers of the sixteenth century for the lack of a biblical basis, sometimes in the face of widespread popular sentiment in favor of them. To argue that these great men had somehow allowed an unscriptural practice to be retained in the church because they were too lazy or indifferent to the truth concerning it was nothing short of slander, especially when you consider that the Reformed and papal theologies of baptism bear no resemblance whatsoever to one another.

But it wasn't just the difference in numbers that got me thinking. What really made an impression on me was the fact that the denominations which had grown out of the Baptist tradition that men like Gill and Bunyan had helped to define, had, for the most part, subsequently abandoned the doctrines of grace. Somewhere along the way, those denominations that had once managed to embrace both Reformed truth concerning redemption and the practice of believer's baptism had later found themselves holding only to the latter. Ultimately, as I will explain in a later chapter, I came to believe that this was no accident, but a natural consequence of attempting to hold these two positions in tandem.

As a member of a Baptist church at the time, these discoveries were a bit unsettling for me. I realized I may have jumped to a conclusion about baptism, accepting for truth what some others had told me about the practice, without really giving due consideration to the views of those who believed otherwise. Though my concerns were still very preliminary at this point, having not yet studied the issue to any great degree on my own, I eventually took them to my Pastor. A committed and lifelong Baptist, he was only too willing and well-prepared to answer my questions, which were still quite basic. But it was in the course of that conversation that this Pastor uttered the words which have become almost an anthem for what I perceive to be the gist of the argument against infant baptism. He told me that he believed that the case for infant baptism was ultimately an 'argument from silence.'

Of course I knew exactly what he meant. It must be admitted by all that there is a certain amount of truth to this statement. Any Reformed Christian who knows Scripture and is honest about it, has to admit that there is no *explicit* instruction concerning the baptism of infants to be found in the New Testament. On the other hand, it is also true that this silence cuts both ways, for the Baptist would also have to admit that there is no explicit injunction *against* baptizing infants.

How much tidier it would be for making the case, either for or against infant baptism, if Luke, in describing the baptisms of entire households in the Book of Acts, had listed the ages of each of the children who received such baptisms, or had simply told us whether the children in such homes were baptized on the basis of their parents' faith, or had expressed biblical faith on their own; or if he had recorded a single instance of a child who had been born into a Christian home who only later received the sign of baptism based upon his own profession of faith. Of course, even better would have been explicit language from one of the Apostles giving instruction as to who were the proper subjects of Christian baptism in the first place.

But all agree that there is no such instruction to be found in the New Testament. At least the Baptist is able to point to the fact that Scripture contains no explicit references to instances of children being baptized, and thereby argue that the Reformed Christian was doing so without explicit biblical authority – engaging in a practice which could only be defended with an 'argument from silence.'

That statement of my Pastor's really got me thinking about the subject, though. There was just something about the words he uttered that I couldn't seem to shake off. The case for infant baptism was merely an argument from silence? Was it really that simple? Could I simply dismiss the views of so many faithful men and women who had come before me by waving my hand and shouting 'argument from silence'? Didn't the Baptist have something a little more positive to offer in the way of a case *against* the practice?

As I undertook to study the issue more intensely, finally taking the time to investigate thoroughly the arguments *for* infant baptism, I eventually came to a startling conclusion – the lack of an explicit biblical command regarding the baptism of infants was a problem not for the Reformed Christian, but for the Baptist! I came to see that there was actually a positive scriptural case to be made for the practice, and came to believe it to be the more biblically faithful and convincing of the two positions.

The notion that silence is a problem for the Baptist, and not for the Reformed, position on this issue is a recurring theme throughout the book. As we proceed I'll demonstrate how the lack of specific language and evidence supporting the Baptist position is the real issue in this debate, requiring the Baptist Christian to jump to conclusions and make pronouncements which are far more problematic in their implications than those the Reformed Christian must make in order to defend infant baptism.

The positive case for infant baptism is a strong one, and the lack of an explicit declaration concerning the proper subjects of baptism, far from detracting from the Reformed position, actually reinforces it. In the end, this debate is just as much about what Scripture does *not* say, as about what it explicitly does say. The Reformed Christian should proudly admit to basing part of his argument for infant baptism on the 'silence' of the New Testament. But in this case, the silence cries out in favor of his position. In this case, as we shall see, the silence is deafening!

Chapter 2

The Covenantal Basis for Baptism

If anyone should know how to define the word 'covenant,' it is O. Palmer Robertson, author of the book *The Christ of the Covenants*.[1] Nevertheless, Robertson writes that trying to define the word 'covenant' is "something like asking for a definition of 'mother.'"[2]

The reason for Robertson's reticence is that the term 'covenant' is an extraordinarily rich one in Scripture, bringing within its scope a variety of ideas and implications, several of which are unique to the biblical notion of a covenant. He does, however, go on to define a covenant as "a bond in blood, sovereignly administered."[3]

This may seem like an odd definition of a term which is familiar to us all in some sense, though we may not use it that often in our everyday conversations. But it is not an odd way to define a *biblical* covenant, because, as we shall see, the primary

---

[1] O. Palmer Robertson, The Christ of the Covenants (Phillipsburg, NJ: P&R, 1980).
[2] Ibid., 3.
[3] Ibid., 4.

usage of the term in the Bible is in reference to God's unilaterally promising certain blessings to His people; and at least in the case of the two most important covenants that we will be looking at closely, sealing them with His blood.

There is no debate about the fact that the notion of 'covenant' is a central one in Scripture. Some would argue that it is *the* central theme around which all of Scripture is organized. That is because the Bible is the record of God's historical work in creation and redemption, which He has accomplished primarily by entering into a series of covenants with certain men (and the groups of people represented by them).

We can identify several different covenants in the Bible. Some are explicitly identified as covenants by the biblical text, while others are nevertheless identifiable by the language used to describe them. Theologians have given them names to identify the men with whom God entered into such covenants. Thus, we have the Adamic, Noahic, Abrahamic, Mosaic, and Davidic covenants, to name some of the more prominent ones.

But the entire biblical record may also be divided into just two comprehensive covenants, from which all of the others flow: the 'covenant of works' and the 'covenant of grace.' The covenant of works refers to the initial covenant under which God related to Adam and Eve in the Garden. God gave them only one restriction – not to eat of the tree of the knowledge of good and evil. Their reward for doing so would be eternal life. However, when Adam and Eve transgressed the covenant of works by eating from the forbidden tree, they lost the gift of eternal life, not only for themselves but for all of their posterity as well. Mankind was now helpless to attain to eternal life on his own.

But God, who is rich in mercy, established a new covenant with Adam and Eve – a covenant of grace – whereby He covered their sin and restored the relationship which had been broken by their disobedience. From that time forward, God has been relating to mankind under this covenant of grace. When the Second Adam, Jesus Christ, fulfilled the requirements of the original covenant of works by living a sinless life and giving that life as an atonement for sin, God graciously provided that the benefits of this work would be available to all who placed their trust in Him.

Thus, the various covenants that we see God establishing with men like Noah, Abraham, Moses and David, are really just the outworking of the more comprehensive plan of redemption embodied in what we call the covenant of grace. Nevertheless, each of these covenants had its own distinctive features and added some new dimension to what had been previously revealed concerning God's ultimate plans for His people.

In this regard, we are primarily concerned with the Abrahamic covenant, because it was there that God began to work His plan of redemption through a particular individual, and gave to him a covenant sign that was to be administered to all of those who would be parties to this covenant. This sign represented God's reminder to them that they were His special possession.

This chapter and the next form the base upon which the argument for infant baptism rests. It is only through a proper understanding of the covenantal nature of baptism and its forerunner, circumcision, that the argument for infant baptism may be fully apprehended and appreciated. Although I have purposely chosen to limit our discussion in this chapter, I also believe that it is unnecessary to go into much more depth than what has been laid out here in order to prove the case. In addition, some passages which might have been discussed under this chapter heading have been reserved for later chapters.

Briefly, the argument here may be broken into three summary headings:

1) God Made an Everlasting Covenant with Abraham;

2) This Covenant is Unfolded and Expanded Upon in the New Covenant Era; and

3) The Sign of the New Covenant is Baptism

God Made an Everlasting Covenant with Abraham

The first eleven chapters of Genesis take us on a whirlwind tour of the early history of man. In rapid succession we learn of God's creation of the universe and mankind, the temptation and fall of man, the first promise of a Redeemer to come, the slaying of Abel by his brother Cain, the story of Noah and the Great Flood, and the scattering of the human race over the face of the earth as a result of the evil design of mankind to make a name for itself by building a tower to the heavens. The span of time covered by these early chapters of the Bible is more than two thousand years.

When we get to chapter twelve, however, the pace of biblical history-telling slows down considerably. It is here that God chooses one individual (Abraham) out of all the earth to become the father of a nation; a nation which was destined to carry the news of God's grace to every one of the people groups just created when He scattered them abroad in the previous chapter.

Specifically, God promised Abraham three things: 1) a land to inhabit; 2) descendants (God would make him "a great nation"); and 3) that he would become a blessing to all nations ("in you all the families of the earth shall be blessed" – Gen. 12:3). But Abraham would first have to take his own family and relocate to a land far away which the Lord would give to him. Abraham complied with the Lord's command and eventually settled in the land of Canaan.

Although Abraham and his extended family were living in the land that God had given to them, they did not yet possess it in any meaningful sense, since they were few in number and surrounded by the Canaanite people who had been in the land for centuries. Nor did Abraham and his wife Sarah, despite being advanced in age, as yet have any children from which to begin to build "a great nation."

So God appeared to Abraham once again. On this occasion, God not only reiterated His promises to Abraham, but also gave him some additional details concerning the scope of them. Not only would Abraham father an heir, but his descendants would one day be as numerous as the stars (Gen. 15:4-5)! Moreover, God laid out in greater detail the boundaries of the land to which Abraham and his descendants were to be the heirs. And it is on this occasion that we read that, "the Lord made a covenant with Abram" (Gen. 15:18).

This covenant was marked by a sacred ceremony in which God directed Abraham to bring a number of animals before Him, and then to cut them in two, down the middle, and place the pieces opposite each other (Gen. 15:9-10). Then, after causing Abraham to fall into a deep sleep, God symbolically passed between the animal pieces in the form of a smoking oven and a burning torch (Gen. 15:17), conveying the message that if He (God) failed to bring these promises to pass, may He be put to death just as these animals had been! In this manner, then, the Abrahamic covenant was confirmed and its promises were sealed by God Himself.

At least thirteen more years passed from the date of this ceremony until God visited Abraham to announce the next phase of His plan to make Abraham a blessing to all nations. During the intervening time period, Abraham and Sarah had attempted to hasten the development of God's plan by having Abraham sire a child by Sarah's maidservant, Hagar. That child, Ishmael, was now thirteen years old; and it had now been twenty-four years from the time God had first appeared to Abraham and called him out of his native country.

But on this visit, God informed them that they were to have a child of their own, born of Sarah, who would be ninety years old on the day that she was to deliver. It was this child, Isaac, who would represent the continuation of the covenant line (Gen. 17:21), the one through whom the promises would continue to descend to the next generation.

Finally, in conjunction with that announcement, God instituted the sign of His covenant with Abraham – circumcision. This sign would mark Abraham and all who came after him (along with their families) as God's special possession. God's words to Abraham are recorded in Genesis 17:

> And God said to Abraham: "As for you, you shall keep My covenant, you and your descendants after you throughout their generations. This is My covenant which you shall keep, between Me and you and your

descendants after you: Every male child among you shall be circumcised; and you shall be circumcised in the flesh of your foreskins, and it shall be a sign of the covenant between Me and you. He who is eight days old among you shall be circumcised, every male child in your generations, he who is born in your house or bought with money from any foreigner who is not your descendant. He who is born in your house and he who is bought with your money must be circumcised, and My covenant shall be in your flesh for an everlasting covenant. And the uncircumcised male child, who is not circumcised in the flesh of his foreskin, that person shall be cut off from his people; he has broken My covenant" (Gen. 17:9-14).

As we move through the biblical case for infant baptism, there are four observations on this particular text that will prove helpful to our discussion along the way:

1) The covenant made with Abraham was an 'everlasting' one, applicable to Abraham's descendants 'throughout their generations;'

2) The sign of this covenant was the rite of circumcision;

3) The sign was to be administered to every male child in Abraham's *house*, which included not only his physical descendants, but all those who would become members of his household by purchase, etc.; and

4) Any male child who failed to receive this rite was 'cut off from his people' (that is, the people of God), for he thereby became a covenant-breaker.

In order to appreciate the significance of this covenant, consider for a moment that throughout the remainder of the Old Testament (and into the New as well), it is this covenant which forms the basis upon which the fulfillment of God's promises to His people is predicated. Over and over God's word tells us that it is in fulfillment of His covenant with Abraham, Isaac, and Jacob that He delivered His people from their groaning under oppression and into the land He had promised them (Ex. 2:24; 6:5; Lev. 26:42; Deut. 9:5; 2 Kings 13:23; Psalm 105:8-11). It is God's *remembrance* of this covenant that prompts Him into action on behalf of His chosen people. He even refers to Himself as the God of Abraham, Isaac, and Jacob when He speaks to Moses at the Burning Bush (Ex. 3:6). And the same appellation is used by the apostle Peter to refer to the God who glorified Jesus Christ after His crucifixion and resurrection (Acts 3:13).

Thus, it is the Abrahamic covenant which lies at the center of God's redemptive work in the flow of biblical history from Genesis 12 onward. It is both a specific form of administration within the context of the all-encompassing covenant of grace, and a separate expression of God's will with its own distinctive characteristics and focus. Moreover, as we will now set out to demonstrate, the Abrahamic covenant comes into its fullest expression with the arrival of the new covenant period.

This Covenant is Unfolded and Expanded Upon in the New Covenant Era

In the opening chapter of Luke's Gospel, the evangelist places the significance of the Abrahamic covenant in full view of the reader. Before he even gets to the birth of Christ, Luke relates two stories which reveal how the promises made to Abraham, Isaac, and Jacob were understood by those who had been awaiting their fulfillment.

The first involves the story of Mary's visit to the home of Elizabeth, the mother-to-be of John the Baptist. Luke tells us that when Elizabeth heard Mary's greeting the unborn John leaped in her womb, causing Elizabeth first, and then Mary, to break out in praise to God for the events to which they were both parties. In her Magnificat, as it has come to be called, Mary praised the Lord for His grace to her and summed up God's provision with these words, "He has helped His servant Israel, in remembrance of His mercy, as he spoke to our fathers, to Abraham and to his seed forever" (Luke 1:54-55).

A few verses later, Zacharias, the father of John the Baptist, recognizes the same reality in relation to the birth of his son, who would be the prophesied forerunner to Christ's appearance upon the scene to save Israel. As he and his family were in the temple for John's circumcision on the eighth day, Zacharias cried out, "Blessed is the Lord God of Israel, for He has visited and redeemed His people ... To perform the mercy promised to our fathers and to remember His holy covenant, the oath which He swore to our father Abraham" (Luke 1:68, 72-73).[4]

Both Mary and Zacharias understood that the long-awaited arrival of Israel's Messiah was in fulfillment of the promises made to "our fathers," and in particular "our father Abraham." Jesus Christ was the hope to which all of the promises given to Abraham and the patriarchs had pointed.

Thus, with Jesus' birth the 'new covenant' era is inaugurated. Jesus' own words testify to this fact, for on the night before He was crucified for the sins of His people, He raised His cup of wine at the Last Supper and pronounced that it henceforth would represent "the new covenant in My blood" (Luke 22:20).

Of course, the existence of a new covenant implies that there was an old one for it to replace. And indeed there was, as the author of the epistle to the Hebrews makes clear in his letter to the first century church. The primary focus of that letter was to proclaim the superiority of Jesus Christ and the new covenant that He brought over the old order of things.

But just what did the writer of the letter mean by the 'old' or 'first' covenant? He identifies it as the covenant God made with Moses (the Mosaic covenant), which because of the work of Christ has now become obsolete, and has been replaced by the new covenant, a covenant which had been foretold by the prophet Jeremiah hundreds of years earlier (Heb. 8:6-13).

The Mosaic covenant, which instituted the ceremonial law into the life of the nation Israel, was only a "shadow of the

---

[4] Given Zacharias' description of it in the verses which follow, the specific 'oath' to which he makes reference is probably the one contained in Genesis 22:16-18, not the covenant ceremony oaths of Genesis chapters 15 and 17. Nevertheless, as you would expect him to do, Zacharias links it to the Abrahamic covenant here (God's "holy covenant"). F.F. Bruce, *New Testament Development of Old Testament Themes*, (Grand Rapids: Eerdmans, 1968), 51.

good things to come" in Christ Jesus (10:1). The system of sacrifices and ritual cleansings that were a part of it pointed the way to something greater and of more benefit – Christ and His finished work on the Cross. He was the fulfillment of all of the expectations symbolized by the shadows and types of the old covenant practices.

Whereas the Mosaic covenant was "symbolic" and "concerned only with foods and drinks, various washings, and fleshly ordinances imposed until the time of reformation" (9:9-10), Christ brought "a better hope, through which we draw near to God" (7:19).

Jesus Christ, who is "worthy of more glory than Moses" (3:3), was a Priest after the order of Melchizedek, not Aaron (7:11); He has become the "surety of a better covenant" (7:22), who does not need to offer up daily sacrifices, as did the priests of old, because "this He did once for all when He offered up Himself" (7:27).

Thus, Christ has "obtained a more excellent ministry, inasmuch as He is also Mediator of a better covenant, which was established on better promises" (8:6). The apostle Paul can even go so far as to say that the old covenant was a "ministry of death," as compared to the "ministry of righteousness" which Christ inaugurated (2 Cor. 3:7-9).

But what about the Abrahamic covenant? Has it too been rendered obsolete by the finished work of Christ in the same way that the Mosaic Covenant has been? The New Testament's answer to that question is an emphatic 'No!' The Abrahamic Covenant, far from being obsolete or set aside, is in the process of being fulfilled in the New Testament age. Indeed, it is unfolding and expanding during the present age as the gospel goes forth to all the world and includes within its sphere people groups who were, prior to the work of Christ, "aliens from the commonwealth of Israel and strangers from the covenants of promise" (Eph. 2:12).

The Abrahamic covenant is in the process of unfolding even now because it is fundamentally a covenant of *election*. That is, it involved God's promise to provide Abraham with heirs; but not just any kind of heirs – *spiritual heirs*. God's covenant with Abraham included the promise that He would be their God as well. And as the New Testament writers confirm many times over, it is only Abraham's *spiritual* descendants who are heirs of the covenant and inheritors of the promises that go with it (Acts 3:25; Rom. 9; Gal. 3:16-4:7; Heb. 6:13-18). Thus, the covenant with Abraham is viewed as being fulfilled in the salvation of God's chosen people, for the promise made to Abraham was the promise of eternal life (Heb. 9:15; 1 John 2:25).

This is why the New Testament writers proclaim the unity and continuity of the church throughout the ages, and apply the various Old Testament designations for the people of God to Christians in the New Testament era (Acts 7:38; Rom. 2:28-29; 9:6, 27-29; Gal. 6:16; 1 Pet. 1:1; 2:9-10; 5:2).

This is why Paul can also say, in view of the fact that the promise to Abraham contained a promise of land as well, that Christians have now inherited the entire world (Rom. 4:13-16). No longer is the gospel message confined to a particular geographical area and people group. Rather, the message of God's salvation is being carried to the corners of the earth, so that ultimately those redeemed by God will come from "every tribe and tongue and people and nation" (Rev. 5:9). In this way, then, Abraham has indeed become the "father of many nations."

With this understanding of the Abrahamic covenant in mind, the significance of Peter's words to the crowd on the day of Pentecost comes into sharp relief. When the crowd in Jerusalem was "cut to the heart" in reaction to Peter's sermon explaining the identity of Jesus as Israel's Messiah, they asked Peter what then they should do about this fact (Acts 2:37). Peter's response to their question was as follows:

> Repent, and let every one of you be baptized in the name of Jesus Christ for the remission of sins; and you shall receive the gift of the Holy Spirit. *For the promise is to you and to your children,* and to all who are afar off, as many as the Lord our God will call (Acts 2:38-39).

The significance of this statement should be obvious. Not only does Peter entreat his listeners to repent of their sins and be *baptized,* but in the same breath (so to speak) he tells them that the *promise* of which he speaks is to them *and their children.* We'll address more directly the way in which baptism has replaced circumcision as the sign of the covenant in the next chapter. But for now it is the second part of Peter's statement that is relevant to our discussion here.

Peter's reference to the 'promise' is a shorthand way of referring to the covenant of grace, and the promise of salvation contained therein; a promise which he has already called upon his hearers to embrace.[5] This is the exact same promise made to Abraham, since that promise is usually referred to in the singular, and the very language used by Peter here is reminiscent of the words of God to Abraham in explicitly including the children of believers in its scope. Moreover, the promise referred to is clearly one concerned with election ("as many as the Lord our God will call").

Some expositors have pointed to the complexity of the context of Peter's words here, since there are clearly a number of things happening in conjunction with Peter's speech, including the outpouring of the Holy Spirit contained in Joel's prophecy which Peter had referred to in his sermon. But however we understand the exact reference to the 'promise' here in verse 39, the resulting implication is the same – the children of those who believe in Christ are included within the scope of God's redemptive plan in the new covenant era.

Needless to say, this is the crux of our argument for infant baptism, so we'll have much more to say about this point before we're through. But for now we'll simply return to the matter at hand, which is the continuation of the Abrahamic covenant in the new covenant dispensation. The bottom line is this: though the sign changes with the coming of the new covenant, the Abrahamic covenant continues unabated, until the last of those for whom Christ gave His life is welcomed into the Kingdom. It is, after all, an everlasting covenant.

---

[5] Joel R. Beeke and Ray B. Lanning, "Unto You, and to Your Children," *The Case for Covenantal Infant Baptism*, ed. Gregg Strawbridge (Phillipsburg, NJ: P&R, 2003), 55.

The Sign of the New Covenant is Baptism

In the days between Jesus' resurrection and His ascension back into heaven, He met with His disciples on multiple occasions, instructing them further on the principles of the Kingdom. It is during this period that Jesus issued what has become known as the 'Great Commission.' Found at Matthew 28:19-20, the words of Jesus were as follows: "Go therefore and make disciples of all the nations, baptizing them in the name of the Father and of the Son and of the Holy Spirit, teaching them to observe all things that I have commanded you; and lo I am with you always, even to the end of the age."

This event marks the inception of the rite of Christian baptism.[6] From this time forward, converts to Christianity were to receive this rite as the sign of initiation into the New Testament church, marking them off from the world at large, and signifying the point at which their lives as disciples of Jesus Christ began.

And, according to the New Testament, it was not many days after the giving of the Great Commission that we see the apostles putting this command into practice (in a big way) at Pentecost, where we read of some three thousand souls being saved and receiving the rite of baptism on that single day (Acts 2:41).

Still, Jesus' command in the Great Commission gives no explicit instructions as to whether or not adult converts were expected to place the mark upon their children, in order to mark them off as belonging to the kingdom as well. This had clearly been the practice in the Old Testament church (with circumcision). But was it also to be the practice of the New Testament church that the sign of the new covenant (baptism) was to be administered to the children of those coming into the kingdom by profession of faith in Christ?

We have already stated that there is no passage in the New Testament containing explicit instructions to this effect, *either for or against* the practice of continuing to give the covenant sign to the children of believers. But there is plenty of reason to

---

[6] In Chapter 4 I will address more fully the issue of how the baptisms of John the Baptist and Jesus' disciples prior to this time differed from the one being instituted here.

believe that this was not only the intention of Jesus in giving the command to baptize, but that it was the actual practice of the Apostles, who were given the task of fulfilling that command.

In addition to the evidence we laid out above in discussing the continuity of the church and the promises given to Abraham which form the basis for the original practice of giving the covenant sign to children, we will look at more evidence supporting the continuation of the practice in the next several chapters as well.

While there is one additional passage that is particularly applicable to the discussion here, its implications and importance to the case are so profound that we have deferred a full discussion of it to the next chapter. That is because Reformed Christians believe it to be one of the strongest pieces of scriptural evidence for maintaining the practice of placing the covenant sign on our children.

Chapter 3

Baptism as the Replacement for Circumcision

The New Testament is clear that circumcision is no longer the rite of entry into membership in God's church, as it had been in Old Testament times. At the Council of Jerusalem, recorded for us in the fifteenth chapter of the book of Acts, the apostles and elders of the church met in Jerusalem to decide what to do about certain men (known as Judaizers) who were spreading the teaching that a person must be circumcised in order to be saved (Acts 15:1).

After discussing the issue, these men issued a decree that was unmistakably clear: circumcision was no longer required for membership in Christ's church, much less a requirement for being saved (of course that had *never* been the case). Paul, indeed, had choice words for those who taught such things, at one point calling them 'the mutilation' (Phil. 3:2).

But if baptism is the sign of the new covenant (as all agree that it is), and circumcision no longer has any religious significance, is it necessarily valid to say that baptism is the New Testament replacement for circumcision? And if so, is that sufficient warrant for assuming that, like circumcision, baptism was designed to be administered to the children of believers? Is baptism, as Reformed Christians argue, 'the circumcision of Christ,' with all of the implications that attend such a statement?

Colossians 2:11-12 seems to answer those questions in the affirmative. That passage reads as follows:

> In Him you were also circumcised with the circumcision made without hands, by putting off the body of sins of the flesh, by the circumcision of Christ, buried with Him in baptism, in which you also were raised with Him through faith in the working of God, who raised Him from the dead.

What is the significance of this passage? This passage demonstrates the essential continuity and progression of the covenant signs, circumcision and baptism. Paul's message to the Colossians that they did not need to undergo physical circumcision because they had received the spiritual reality of it, which was confirmed and sealed at their baptism, presents baptism as the sign to which circumcision was ultimately pointing. Indeed, as we will develop further in the next few pages, it identifies baptism as the 'circumcision of Christ.' In this way, then, baptism is set forth as the replacement for circumcision in the New Covenant era.

This is not the only understanding of this text, however. So as we move on to the task of unpacking this passage and presenting our case more thoroughly, we will do so primarily by interacting with an alternative understanding of it. The common Baptist charge against the interpretation of Colossians 2:11-12 we have just laid out is that Reformed Christians have failed to properly distinguish between the physical and spiritual references to circumcision and baptism in that passage.

The Baptist argument goes like this: Reformed Christians have made two fundamental mistakes in interpreting Colossians

2:11-12. First, they have traditionally interpreted the reference to baptism in verse 12 as referring to physical baptism, when it is actually a reference to spiritual baptism (i.e., regeneration). Second, they have incorrectly associated the reference to the 'circumcision of Christ' with the reference to baptism immediately following, when it should be seen as linked to the preceding clauses, particularly the reference to the 'circumcision made without hands.' The combination of these two errors, so the argument goes, has the effect of changing the meaning of the phrase 'circumcision of Christ' from being another way to refer to spiritual circumcision (as with 'the circumcision made without hands') to providing a convenient way to say that the physical rite of baptism is the 'circumcision of Christ.'

The upshot of this argument is that the Baptist believes that this passage, if properly understood as containing no reference to physical baptism, teaches that it is *spiritual circumcision* (i.e., regeneration), not physical baptism, that has replaced *physical circumcision* as the rite of entry into the church.[1] In other words, it is only those who have been spiritually circumcised (regenerated) who are members of the church and are thus entitled to receive the rite of baptism. The obvious effect of this understanding is to rule out the possibility of baptizing infants.

This is a clever argument. But there are at least three serious problems with it. First, the argument just laid out completely misconstrues the Reformed position on this passage. The Reformed Christian is not at all dependent upon a reading of the text which equates the reference to baptism in verse 12 with the *physical* rite. It may be true that most Reformed commentators have interpreted the reference in that way, but as I will show in a moment, even this interpretive decision does not affect the ultimate argument concerning this passage.

Nor are we dependent upon a construction of the passage which severs the reference to the circumcision of Christ from

---

[1] See, e.g., Thomas R. Schreiner, "Baptism in the Epistles: An Initiation Rite for Believers," *Believer's Baptism: Sign of the New Covenant in Christ*, eds. Thomas R. Schreiner & Shawn D. Wright (Nashville: B&H Academic, 2006), 75-79.

that of the one made without hands. Rather, it is the sense of the entire passage which gives rise to the Reformed affirmation that "baptism is the circumcision of Christ."

Second, even if we were to grant the Baptist understanding of the two clauses in question, it would not lead to the interpretation which is urged upon the passage as a whole. Even then the text simply does not say what the Baptist claims it says. With either construction of the passage, the most natural interpretive reading is still the Reformed one.

The best way to demonstrate this is to go through the passage in detail. In order to do so, we have broken the passage down into the six clauses or thought-units which flow naturally from the text. But it is even more helpful to look at the entire passage as three units of thought consisting of two clauses each. The advantages of this approach will become apparent as we proceed.

"(1) In Him you were also circumcised (2) with the circumcision made without hands"

Paul begins by telling the Colossian Christians that they did not need physical circumcision because they were complete in Christ by virtue of their *spiritual* circumcision (regeneration). Remember that the context is Paul's admonition to the Colossians that they need not succumb to the false teachings that the Judaizers were spreading, one of which was that circumcision was necessary in order to become a Christian. The Christian has all he needs in Christ Himself. He has received the 'circumcision made without hands.' Thus, when Paul says that in Christ they *were* circumcised, he is telling his largely Gentile audience that they did not need to undergo physical circumcision because it no longer had any religious significance in the new covenant age.

"(3) By putting off the body of the sins of the flesh, (4) by the circumcision of Christ"

These two clauses represent a transition between the reference to circumcision in #2 and the reference to baptism in #5. They form a point of contact between the Old Testament rite of circumcision and the New Testament rite of baptism. First, Paul interjects a statement about how the Colossians had put off "the body of the sins of the flesh." This presumably happened at the same time they were "circumcised with the circumcision made without hands."

But Paul's choice of language here is interesting for two reasons. First, he uses a phrase which evokes images of physical circumcision, where the foreskin of the body is "put off." In the case of the 'circumcision made without hands,' however, it is the entire body (of the sins of the flesh) which is put off. Thus, the superiority of spiritual circumcision over physical circumcision is once again affirmed by Paul.

Second, and even more interesting, is that in reaffirming this superiority, Paul has now shifted to discussing the *effects* of this spiritual circumcision with the same language he ascribes to the effects of spiritual baptism in Romans 6:4-6. Indeed, the language and essence of that passage and the one under consideration here are strikingly similar. The believer's victory over the power of sin comes about as a result of his union with Christ, which is symbolized by circumcision in the old dispensation, and by baptism in the new.

All of which makes it more likely that Paul is using the phrase "by the circumcision of Christ" (#4) as a lead-in to discuss baptism (#5), rather than as another reference limited solely to the act of spiritual circumcision, and thereby harkening back to the reference in #2. This is not to deny that the phrase contains that sense of meaning as well, but only to assert that it is more natural to read it as looking forward within the passage, not backward. To say that the phrase is simply another way of referring to the "circumcision made without hands," seems to add a layer of redundancy and break the general flow of the passage, which is moving from circumcision to baptism.

Thus, it seems to me that the phrase "the circumcision of Christ" serves a dual purpose here. It carries the discussion of circumcision all the way from the Old Testament physical rite (#1) into its New Testament counterpart, baptism, and it also affirms that both of these ordinances come from, and find their fulfillment in, Christ.

The 'circumcision of Christ,' then, has both physical and spiritual dimensions. It is faith in Christ which brings about spiritual circumcision, and it is the physical rite of baptism which is the sign and seal of that reality. Therefore, as baptism has replaced circumcision by the direct command of Christ Himself, it is appropriate to speak of baptism as the 'circumcision of Christ.'

I am jumping ahead of our discussion just a bit here, but we can paraphrase the entirety of Paul's statement to the Colossians as follows, "You received the equivalent of your physical circumcision (#1) when you were baptized (#5), having already received the inward, spiritual reality of it (#2) and its effects (#3) when you placed your trust in Christ (#6). Thus, you have received the only circumcision that has any continuing validity – the circumcision of Christ (#4)."

"(5) Buried with Him in baptism, (6) in which you also were raised with Him through faith in the working of God, who raised Him from the dead."

Paul finally connects circumcision with baptism by asserting that, just as God raised Christ from the dead, so has He raised the Colossian Christians from spiritual death by granting them faith, all of which was confirmed and pictured at their baptism. Thus, Paul speaks of both physical (#5) and spiritual (#6) baptism here, just as he had spoken of both physical (#1) and spiritual (#2) circumcision at the beginning of the passage. In this way, then, the entire text exhibits a certain poetic structure, not uncommon to Paul or the other biblical writers.

On the other hand, Baptists often assert that the reference to baptism in #5 above should be understood to refer only to spiritual, not physical, baptism. Thus, #5 and #6 are not two separate thought-units, but one, both describing the work of regeneration.

That is certainly a possibility. But if that were the case, it would raise a number of ancillary questions. First, why would Paul mention baptism at all in this context? If the reference to baptism is merely another way to speak of regeneration, then what does it add to the passage that has not already been stated in the references to the circumcision made without hands, or the circumcision of Christ?

Second, since this argument is used to make the general case that spiritual baptism has replaced physical circumcision, isn't the force of such an argument to imply that physical baptism is not a requirement at all? But it was commanded by the Lord Himself! The fact that such an ordinance does not save is not an excuse for despising or neglecting it. We should always be mindful that these are Christ's sacraments, not ours, and we have no right to do with them (or without them) as we please.

Finally – and here is the crux of the matter – we must ask if it really makes any difference to the general thrust of the passage if Paul is referring to physical or spiritual baptism in the first part of verse 12? Even if we were to assume that the first half of verse 12 is a reference to spiritual baptism, it still would not mean what the Baptist asserts. After all, it is a given that the Colossian Christians had received spiritual circumcision, and if so, then they would have been baptized. Their physical baptism would be assumed by Paul.

Nor would the fact that Paul ends with a reference to spiritual baptism after beginning with physical circumcision mean that spiritual baptism has replaced physical circumcision as the sign of the New Covenant. Rather, it is simply an effective method for demonstrating the superiority of the spiritual reality over the physical rite, and of baptism over circumcision. In both cases, the former is to be preferred. But physical baptism is not thereby done away with.

The point here is that the general thrust of the Colossians passage is that circumcision and baptism are equivalent rites. Even if the baptism being spoken of here is spiritual, then clearly spiritual circumcision is meant to be equivalent to spiritual baptism, since both refer to the act of regeneration. And if spiritual circumcision is equivalent to spiritual baptism, then to what would physical circumcision be equivalent? The answer, of course, is obvious.

But if the baptism spoken of here is physical (as we assert), then it is clearly brought up for the purpose of demonstrating that it was the Colossians' baptism which signified and sealed this circumcision of the heart. Either way, the point is the same.

Which brings us to the third problem with the Baptist interpretation of this text – it unnecessarily complicates the passage. As we have just argued, allowing our interpretation of the text to hinge upon a determination of whether the phrase 'circumcision of Christ' is forward or backward looking, or whether the reference to baptism is physical or spiritual, is a prime example of missing the forest for the trees.

The simplest and most natural understanding of a passage is always to be preferred in the absence of solid evidence that there is more to the wording than meets the eye. But I do not believe that to be the case here. Clearly, Paul means to link the two rites of baptism and circumcision together by means of this passage. He speaks of them in the same breath, as it were. Read the passage above several times and then decide for yourself which interpretation of the text, Baptist or Reformed, seems to flow most naturally from the words.

Let me be clear – I am not making light of attempts at in-depth biblical exegesis, or interpretations that rely upon lexical considerations, etc. On the contrary, we just spent several pages attempting our own in-depth analysis of the passage under consideration here. Rather, I'm merely arguing that I don't believe such considerations as we've mentioned make any ultimate difference to the general thrust or meaning of this passage, and that at least some expositors have probably raised such issues in an effort to divert attention from that meaning, or to evade its force altogether.

The Old Testament rite of circumcision was a bloody sign that pointed forward to the once-for-all sacrifice of Jesus Christ on the Cross of Calvary. Having been fulfilled, it was Christ

Himself who instructed His Apostles to administer the new sign of baptism, which now looks back to that finished work. Thus, we may say that it is a simple statement of fact that 'baptism is the circumcision of Christ.'

Baptist Counter-Arguments

As we have already pointed out, there is no real debate about the fact that baptism is the sign of the new covenant, or even that baptism has replaced circumcision *in that sense*. Rather, the debate centers around what implications may legitimately be drawn from those facts, and whether or not there are new factors to consider in properly administering the sign of baptism.

Baptists agree that the sign of the new covenant is baptism, but they would depart from the practice of the Old Testament church by withholding that sign from the children of believers until they are old enough to make a credible profession of faith on their own. But how do Baptists justify such a departure? They usually do so with one of two very similar, and related, arguments.

The first is the argument that the meaning and significance of the rite of baptism is different from that of circumcision. In other words, they argue that the nature of the sign has changed. They assert that circumcision was simply a mark of national identity in the Old Testament church, with no real spiritual significance to it. Those who were born into the nation of Israel or were brought into it by some other means were given the sign to identify themselves as Israelites, but not necessarily as a reflection of any spiritual reality concerning their individual status within the corporate people of God in the Old Testament period.

The problem with this argument is that the New Testament explicitly contradicts it. In Paul's epic treatise on salvation by grace in the third and fourth chapters of Romans, he speaks of Abraham's having been justified by faith before he was circumcised, and then adds, "And he received the sign of circumcision, *a seal of the righteousness of the faith which he had while still uncircumcised*, that he might be the father of all those who believe" (Rom. 4:11).

Thus, any argument that the significance of the sign has changed from its Old Testament usage must fail, for Paul makes it abundantly clear that circumcision served the same function as baptism does in the New Testament period – as a sign and seal of the righteousness of faith. And yet, as we know, circumcision was applied even to those who were unable to make any such profession of faith on their own.

The second argument that is frequently advanced by Baptists is that the nature of the church has changed, so that only those who are truly redeemed, and can make their own profession to that effect, are to be a part of the New Testament church. This, of course, is very similar to the argument against the Reformed interpretation of Colossians 2:11-12 that we outlined above. But it is usually the thirty-first chapter of the Old Testament prophecy of Jeremiah to which Baptists look for support of this idea.

In that prophecy, Jeremiah announced to Israel and Judah that the day was coming when the Lord would make a new covenant with them. That covenant would be even better than the one which He had made with their fathers because a) it would be unbreakable; b) it would include the law being written on the hearts of its participants; and c) all such participants would have their sins forgiven, for they would all "know the Lord" (Jer. 31:31-34).

Several observations about this passage are in order. First, there can be no doubt about the fact that we are in the period embraced by Jeremiah's prophecy, as Jesus and the New Testament writers confirm for us in multiple places (Luke 22:20; 1 Cor. 11:25; 2 Cor. 3:6; Heb. 8:8, 13; 9:15; 12:24). But the passage does not teach that the 'visible' church of the new covenant era will be composed only of true believers. Rather, it speaks to the superiority of the new covenant over that of the old, a fact which we have already pointed out at length.

Jeremiah's prophecy asserts a qualitative difference between the work of the Holy Spirit in the lives of New Testament believers when compared to those in the Old Testament period. And there is certainly a change in the makeup of the visible people of God as the New Testament church expands beyond the borders of Israel and loses the national character that was so much a part of the Old Testament era. But there is no indication in Jeremiah's words that the New Testament church would be given supernatural power to discern true biblical faith from false in every single case, or that the rules for membership in the church were to be changed so as to exclude those who were previously included (i.e., the children of believers).

Moreover, the Baptist view of Jeremiah's prophecy fails to take into account the clear instruction of the New Testament that the church in this age can, and will, contain within its midst those who are not regenerate at all. And it is also clear that some of these false believers will have given credible evidence of having true biblical faith at some point in time.

This is why we still see, even after the New Testament church is well underway, abundant warnings to watch out for those who are wolves in sheep's clothing and are told that some who have gone out "from us" were not truly "of us." One passage that is particularly applicable to our discussion here is Hebrews 10:28-29, which reads as follows:

> Anyone who has rejected Moses' law dies without mercy on the testimony of two or three witnesses. Of how much worse punishment, do you suppose, will he be thought worthy who has trampled the Son of God underfoot, counted the blood of the covenant by which he was sanctified a common thing, and insulted the Spirit of grace?

This passage, which comes from the very same epistle which so strenuously argues for the superiority of the new covenant, proves that even some who have been sanctified (set apart) by the blood of the covenant, a phrase which implies membership in the church and participation in its benefits, may yet end up trampling the Son of God underfoot and insulting the Spirit of grace. Richard Pratt points out that the three objects in focus here – the Son of God, the blood of the covenant, and the Spirit of grace – are all new covenant features, and that this passage demonstrates the New Testament's expectation that some genuine participants will turn out to be covenant breakers.[2]

At this point it is also necessary to make note of an important distinction in our theological language. When we speak of the covenant people of God we tend most often to use the term in reference to the "visible" people of God; that is, those who have received the covenant sign and are a part of the visible covenant community on earth (OT Israel and the NT church).

But it should be pointed out that, because the covenant of grace is a covenant of election, only those to whom the promise of election applies (the "invisible" church) are truly covenant members. The promises of grace contained in the covenant are made only to the elect, but the sign of the covenant, by God's express command, is administered to some who are not a part of His *true* covenant people. In His sovereignty, God has determined the bounds for both groups: those to whom His covenant promise applies, and those who are entitled to receive the sign.

As a result, it is improper to speak of the covenant as a conditional one, as if it was a mere offer of grace to all who receive the sign, but conditioned upon their subsequent response in faith. Nor is it an actual bestowal of grace upon all who are baptized, with the recipient having the ultimate ability to resist the grace offered therein. Rather, the promise contained in the covenant is a *promise to save*; and it is effectual for all to whom God has extended it.

The notion of a conditional covenant is the root error of the contemporary heresy known as the 'Federal Vision.' By positing a covenant with promises that are conditioned upon the actions of sinful human beings, the men who teach this modern version of a very old lie pervert the Bible's teaching that grace within the covenant is particular and efficacious. The natural end to which their faulty theological premise leads those within this movement is a denial of the doctrine of justification by grace alone, through faith alone.

---

[2] Richard L. Pratt, Jr., "Infant Baptism in the New Covenant," *The Case for Covenantal Infant Baptism*, 170.

It is true that some Reformed theologians have spoken of the covenant of grace as conditional in the perfectly biblical sense that faith is the "necessary means by which God bestows his salvation upon the elect sinner, without which God does not save the elect sinner, and which God himself works within the heart of the elect sinner." But it is not, as these purveyors of strange doctrines teach, a covenant whose promise *depends upon* the act of the sinner, either in believing or doing the works which flow from faith. Faith and obedience are themselves part of the promise of the covenant, and are graciously given to all those whom God has elected to salvation.[3]

Because it is God Himself who fulfills all the terms of the covenant, including providing the faith which is the instrumental cause of our justification, the covenant of grace is thus properly understood as an unconditional one. In that sense, then, there are none who actually "break" the covenant, since they were never parties to it in the first place. Nevertheless, given the language of Hebrews 10, it seems fair to apply the term "covenant breakers" to those who have received the covenant sign and have tasted of the blessings which accompany membership in the church, but go on to reject the Lord who provides those blessings.

Based upon the New Testament evidence, we must conclude that Baptists have misunderstood and misapplied Jeremiah's prophecy concerning the new covenant. The time will indeed come when the church of Jesus Christ will be composed of only those who have been truly sanctified by *His* blood, but that time is not yet here. William Shisko underscores the importance of this point in the following way:

> Can our Baptist friends point to one church that is composed only of the regenerate? This is the Achilles heel of any Baptist view. In the new heavens and the new earth, when the new covenant will be consummated, only

---

[3] For an excellent presentation of the subject matter under discussion here, see David J. Engelsma, *The Covenant of God and the Children of Believers: Sovereign Grace in the Covenant* (Grandville, MI: Reformed Free Publishing Association, 2005). The material quoted in this paragraph is from page 174 of that work.

the elect will compose the church. Until then, even the best of Baptist churches and any other Christian church will be composed of both regenerate and unregenerate people. Hence, there are stern warnings addressed to people in the church (e.g., Heb. 6:4-6; 10:26-36). There are calls to examine ourselves, to see *whether* we are in the faith (2 Cor. 13:5). Paul has doubts about those in Galatia who had professed faith and been baptized, but were falling back into legalism (Gal. 4:19-20). Simon the sorcerer "believed" (outwardly) and was baptized (Acts 8:13), yet he was hardly regenerate (see Acts 8:21-23). People left the church because they never were truly a part of it (1 John 2:19). Whole churches were threatened with Christ's judgments because they had left their first love, given in to sexual immorality and false doctrine, and become lukewarm; they had the reputation of being alive, but they were dead (Rev. 2, 3). These are new covenant realities, and they are hardly the realities of a fully regenerate church![4]

At the heart of the issue, then, is our understanding of the nature of the church. Has its very essence changed, so that it no longer includes children, as it had all throughout the period leading up to resurrection of Christ? Are the children of believers now on the 'outside,' to be viewed by those on the inside only as potential Christians?

We'll have much more to say about this issue in the next chapter. But for now we want to ask a more fundamental question that is raised by such an argument. Is God's covenant (and thus His grace) *more restrictive* now than in the dispensation prior to Christ's coming? Was it His intention to usher in an age that now excluded an entire class of people that had previously been included in the visible community of the church? If we are to believe the Baptist argument that children are no longer

---

[4] William Shishko, "A Better Case for Infant Baptism," *New Horizons in the Orthodox Presbyterian Church* (March 2008), 7, 13.

entitled to the covenant sign, and the privileges that attend thereto, that is the only conclusion that we could draw.

But, of course, the evidence from the New Testament reveals just the opposite. The tendency in the New Testament age is to *include* groups of people who used to be on the outside.[5] The most obvious example of this is the inclusion of the Gentiles into the church. It was Christ's work which resulted in the breaking down of the middle wall of partition which had previously separated them from God's covenant community. And now the gospel is going forth to all the earth, having previously been restricted to a relatively small land mass in the Middle East.

We live in an age of *greater grace*, not lesser.[6] And the very nature of baptism demonstrates that fact, given that the sign of the covenant, which had previously been reserved only for males, has been changed to allow for its administration to both males and females.

Which brings us to the real question – if the rules of the Kingdom have changed in such a fundamentally significant way, then wouldn't we expect to be able to point to something a little more concrete and explicit in God's Word as warrant for making such a change? The point of demonstrating the connection between circumcision and baptism is to show that, absent an explicit removal of the command to administer the sign to covenant children, we are on safe ground continuing the practice that *has* explicit divine authority.

Those who argue against the practice of infant baptism like to say that the lack of an explicit positive command to baptize infants gives the death knell to such an idea. However, in so arguing, the Baptist has merely substituted a *different* argument from silence – the argument that God no longer intends for the sign of His covenant promise to be administered to the children of believers in the new covenant era. But there is simply no language in the New Testament to support such a view.

---

[5] Dennis Johnson, "Infant Baptism: How My Mind Has Changed," *IIIM Magazine Online*, vol. 3, number 24 (June 11-17, 2001), 11. Accessed May 25, 2008. Online: http://thirdmill.org/newfiles/den_johnson/TH.Johnson.Baptism.pdf.

[6] I am grateful to my own Pastor, James R. Megchelsen, for regularly reminding the congregation of this fact.

Rather, such an argument reflects a dispensationalist view of the Bible. Dispensationalism may be defined as both an interpretive approach to the Bible and as a movement which has been ascendant in American Christianity for the last 100 years. Dispensationalists tend to view the work of God in the Old and New Testament periods as quite distinct in character and design. They would view the basic march of biblical history as being "interrupted" by Christ's rejection and crucifixion, and thereby being replaced by a new dispensation centered on a different people group, the Gentiles (all those of non-Jewish origin). At a later point in time, however, God will return to His original plan of setting up an earthly kingdom with Jesus at the helm, and with those of Jewish racial origin once again at the center of that kingdom.

Thus, dispensationalists argue for a basic *discontinuity* between the Old and New Testaments, and between the people of God in those two dispensations. In this scheme, then, the Abrahamic covenant does not find its fulfillment in the new covenant that Christ instituted, but is merely postponed and temporarily supplanted by the latter.

The problems with this view are too numerous to address here, but suffice it to say that it is at odds with the historic Reformed and Christian understanding of the biblical record. Indeed, we have already laid out in great detail the New Testament's witness to the continuation of the church community and the redemptive plan of God. Jesus' own words testify to the fact that His Kingdom was not of this world, but that the very purpose for which He came was to give His life as a ransom for many.

Of course, I am well aware that few who occupy the pews of the average church in America today could articulate the tenets of such a view, even if they be in a church which formally subscribes to the dispensational creed. Nor are all of those who hold to a Baptist view of the sacraments committed to the dispensational interpretation of Scripture. But the basic emphasis upon the discontinuity of the Bible is rampant within the church today. Many of those who worship in American churches today are *de facto* dispensationalists, in that they act as though the Abrahamic covenant has been (at least partially) abrogated, and that the people of God in the new covenant era relate to Him under an entirely new set of rules.

An interesting example of this tendency occurred in a Bible study that I was leading in our home a few years ago. After I explained the dispensationalist view of the Bible to the group, everyone to a person stated that they had never heard of such a notion and didn't think they knew anyone who adhered to it either. But when we got to the subject of baptism, one of the men in the group asked me, incredulously, to show him where in the Bible we were instructed to baptize infants. When I answered, "Genesis 17," he hesitated for a moment, and then replied, "Show me where it says so in the *New* Testament."

Of course, Genesis 17 says nothing about baptism, but it does state *explicitly* that the sign of God's covenant care and protection is to be administered to the children of believers.

I'm quite certain that this godly man from my study group is not a full-blown dispensationalist, and that such would also be the case with most of those who fill the pews of the average Baptist church. But his reaction exemplifies all too clearly the tendency in today's church to emphasize the discontinuity of Scripture, and to demand explicit New Testament reaffirmation of principles laid down in the Old Testament.

To be sure, a great number of things did change with the coming of Christ and the arrival of the new covenant age, but they changed for the better, not for the worse! The late John Murray has summarized our argument here well:

> If infants are excluded now, it cannot be too strongly emphasised that this change implies a complete reversal of the earlier divinely instituted practice. So we must ask: do we find any hint or intimation of such reversal in either the Old or New Testament? More pointedly, does the New Testament revoke or does it provide any intimation of revoking so expressly authorised a principle as that of the inclusion of infants in the covenant and their participation

in the covenant sign and seal? This practice has been followed, by divine authority, in the administration of the covenant of grace for some two thousand years. Has it been discontinued? Our answer to these questions must be that we find no evidence of revocation. In view of the fact that the new covenant is based upon and is the unfolding of the Abrahamic covenant, in view of the basic identity of meaning attaching to circumcision and baptism, in view of the unity and continuity of the covenant grace administered in both dispensations, we can affirm with confidence that evidence of revocation or repeal is mandatory if the practice or principle has been discontinued under the New Testament.

In the absence of such evidence of repeal we conclude that the administering of the sign and seal of the covenant to the infant seed of believers is still in operation and has perpetual divine warrant.[7]

Some would have us believe that God intended to exclude our children from His covenant community in this age of greater grace, despite the lack of any positive biblical evidence demonstrating such a change of heart on God's part. In the matter of infant baptism – dare I say it? – that is the real argument from silence.

---

[7] John Murray, *Christian Baptism*, (Phillipsburg, NJ: P&R, 1980), 49-50.

Chapter 4

Jesus' Blessing of the Little Children

As a Ruling Elder in the Orthodox Presbyterian Church (OPC), I have the responsibility and privilege, along with my fellow elders, of conducting examinations for church membership. It is a joy to hear the stories of how God has brought people in different circumstances and from different backgrounds to saving faith in Jesus Christ.

Some time ago we interviewed a family which had come from a church that adhered to the doctrines of grace, but practiced believer's baptism. As we began to wrap up our conversation and asked if they had any questions, the wife remarked that she agreed with everything that the OPC confessed, except for infant baptism. Then she summed up her reason for believing as she did in these words, "When I look at the New Testament, I see Jesus only *blessing* the little children, and only adults being baptized."

There it is again – the accusation that the silence of the New Testament with regard to these two observations dooms the case for infant baptism. Since the Gospel accounts do not specifically reference Jesus or His disciples baptizing infants, but only blessing them, so the argument goes, there is no warrant for infant baptism. Similarly, since there are no explicit references to infants being baptized in the book of Acts (or elsewhere in the New Testament), the argument for infant baptism is once again dismissed as an 'argument from silence.'

We'll cover the first issue (Jesus' blessing of the little children) in this chapter, and the second (only adults being baptized) in the next.

As to the first issue, the relevant passages appear below:

> Then they brought little children to Him, that He might touch them; but the disciples rebuked those who brought them. But when Jesus saw it, He was greatly displeased and said to them, "Let the little children come to Me, and do not forbid them; for of such is the kingdom of God. Assuredly, I say to you, whoever does not receive the kingdom of God as a little child will by no means enter it." And He took them up in His arms, laid His hands on them, and blessed them. (Mark 10:13-16; cf. Matt. 19:13-15; Luke 18:15-17).

> At that time the disciples came to Jesus, saying, "Who then is the greatest in the kingdom of heaven?" Then Jesus called a little child to Him, set him in the midst of them, and said, "Assuredly, I say to you, unless you are converted and become as little children, you will by no means enter the kingdom of heaven. Therefore whoever humbles himself as this little child is the greatest in the kingdom of heaven. Whoever receives one little child like this in My name receives Me. But whoever causes one of these little ones who believe in Me to sin, it would be better for him if a millstone were hung around his neck, and he were drowned in the depth of the sea." (Matt. 18:1-6; cf. Luke 9:46-48)

Some years ago I listened to a debate on the subject of baptism between two well-known Bible teachers and authors, one Baptist and one Reformed. The Baptist author presented his case first, and a good chunk of his remarks were devoted to enumerating the various passages that he believed Reformed Christians relied upon to build their case for infant baptism, and attempting to demonstrate that they did not actually offer support for the doctrine. He included the passages now under consideration, with the observation that they only addressed the heart attitude that was required of anyone who would come to Christ for salvation (childlike faith), and nothing more.

When it was time for the Reformed author to respond, to my surprise he simply agreed with his colleague about these particular passages and moved on to what he considered to be the more important items for debate. Now perhaps we can appreciate the desire to use the limited time allowed for in a debate to focus on the most substantive disagreements at issue, but are the words and actions of Jesus in these verses really that irrelevant to our discussion?

Though I have the utmost respect for this Reformed author, I must admit that I found it astonishing that he could so easily dismiss these passages as if they had *nothing whatsoever* to do with the subject of infant baptism. I'll grant that they do not speak to the subject of baptism *per se*. But what could be more relevant to the issue than a direct statement from Jesus Himself as to the place of children in the Kingdom?

A few observations about the passages quoted above are in order:

1) These two passages record two separate incidents. The first records the remarks of Jesus in reaction to His disciples' refusal to let the people bring their young children to Him, while the second records His remarks in answer to a question posed by His disciples as to who was the greatest in the kingdom. Thus, although the passages are very similar to one another, and are often considered together, it is only the first that involves the issue of Jesus' blessing of the children;

2) The little children that were being presented to Jesus for blessing were infants, as disclosed in Luke's parallel account (Luke 18:15); so there is no chance that He was making reference to children who were of a sufficient age to profess faith in Him on their own;

3) Jesus remarks that "of such [little children] is the kingdom of God";

4) In the second passage, Jesus equates receiving the little child in His name with receiving Him; and

5) Jesus refers to the child in the second passage as one who "believes" in Him.

With these background facts in mind, what are we to make of the statement that because Jesus only blessed little children, but did not baptize them, that such 'blessing' passages detract from the case for infant baptism? We offer the following three points in response, which show this argument to be without any force whatsoever.

First, the short answer to this argument is that Christian baptism didn't begin until after Jesus' death and resurrection. The rite of Christian baptism was instituted by Jesus in His Great Commission, where He instructed His Apostles to go and make disciples of all nations and baptize them in the name of the Father, Son and Holy Spirit (Matt. 28:19).

Both John the Baptist and the disciples of Jesus baptized individuals during the three and one-half year interval between Jesus' own baptism and His death on the Cross. But each of these baptisms was clearly preparatory in nature, as confirmed by the fact that they were baptisms of repentance reserved for those in Israel, whereas the Christian baptism that Jesus instituted was extended to all nations.[1]

Indeed, Acts 19:1-5 proves that the baptism of John was not equivalent to the Christian baptism that succeeded it, since Paul re-baptized those in the church at Ephesus who had received only John's baptism. Even the baptism that Jesus' disciples administered in His name prior to the Great Commission was distinct from the one which succeeded it, since Christian baptism looks back to the finished work (death and resurrection) of Christ (Rom. 6:3-4; Col. 2:11-12).

Moreover, lest I miss an opportunity to turn the 'argument from silence' refrain against those who so frequently employ it to

---

[1] William Hendriksen, *New Testament Commentary: Matthew* (Grand Rapids: Baker, 1973), 146.

deny the practice of infant baptism, I should point out that the New Testament nowhere says that infants were *not* the recipients of either of these baptisms. Yet I will grant that the best evidence suggests that they were not, but only for the reasons I just stated – that these were baptisms of repentance and preparation, and were not equivalent to Christian baptism, which replaced the Old Testament rite of circumcision.

Second, we must assume that Jesus' words and actions in these two passages had real meaning and significance. Frankly, it is mystifying to me that someone would use the argument of Jesus' blessing the little children, even if couched in terms of His *only* blessing them, as an argument *against* infant baptism. Such an argument seems to miss the significance of Jesus' actions altogether.

What, after all, is the purpose of Jesus' blessing them and of saying that "of such is the kingdom of God," if not to announce to the whole world that children are a part of His visible community on earth, and are thus entitled to its benefits and protection. Are we to suppose that when Jesus said, "Whoever receives one little child like this in My name receives Me," that He meant to add the qualifying words, "Of course, you may wait to receive the child until he is old enough to profess his own faith in Me"?

What about Jesus' reference to the little ones who *believe* in Him? If Jesus had merely meant to stress the necessity of childlike faith in these passages (as many Baptists argue), would He not have used an adult with childlike faith to emphasize the point?[2] But He did not do so, because both of these passages are concerned about the treatment of little children, not adults! Read them again (if necessary), and you will see that there is simply no way to allegorize these two accounts (particularly the first) in order to render them applicable only to adults, even if limited to those adults with 'childlike faith.' There is indeed a message to adults in both passages, but Jesus is concerned here with children, and He demonstrates His love toward them by

---

[2] Shishko, 7.

blessing them, and by warning all those who would refuse their reception into His Church that they are thereby refusing to receive Him.

Third, there is plenty of additional evidence to prove that children were considered a part of the New Testament church, just as they had been in the Old Testament dispensation. For starters, Paul addressed children directly in his letters to the Ephesians (6:1) and Colossians (3:20). They were considered amongst the 'saints' to whom both letters were directed.

One of the most important passages in the entire New Testament concerning the issue at hand is 1 Corinthians 7:14. In that verse Paul declares that, whereas the offspring of unbelieving parents is considered 'unclean,' the child of at least one believing parent is 'holy.' Does this mean that believers have a guarantee that their children are elect and will be brought to faith in Christ in due time? No, it does not. Both Scripture and personal experience confirm that this is not the case. But it does mean that they are, in God's eyes, of a different character and standing before Him. They are considered a part of His visible community on earth (the church), bearing testimony to His grace and work amongst His creatures, and thus are to be marked off from the unbelieving world around them. Of course, the way in which this is accomplished is by the administration of the covenant sign – baptism.

But that is not the whole picture either, for the children of believing parents are not merely placed in a more advantageous setting whereby their chances to be brought to faith are greater by virtue of their being exposed to the means of grace (the preaching of the word and the sacraments). It is God alone who gives faith, and the doctrine of His sovereignty in election is just as applicable within the covenant community as it is on the outside. *However, it is not primarily from the great mass of people in the world that God chooses those whom He will bring to faith.* Rather, He has promised to be gracious to our children, and so He has seen fit to build His church primarily from within – by drawing our children (and theirs, and so on) in grace unto Himself. Scripture and personal experience also confirm this as fact for us.

Finally, it bears repeating from the last chapter that we live in an era of greater grace, not lesser. It is hard to imagine any Hebrew Christian reading the epistle to the Hebrews in the first few decades of the New Testament era and agreeing with the author about the superiority of the new covenant, while being told at the same time that his children were no longer subject to its blessings and protections. But that is precisely where we find ourselves if we accept the premise that infants in the present day are not entitled to receive Christian baptism.

The fact that so many of our Baptist brethren have replaced the rite of baptizing their infant children with 'baby dedication' ceremonies is, in my judgment, a sign that they too are uncomfortable with the full implications of this position. But I find it difficult to embrace a practice which finds no warrant in Scripture, especially given the abundant warnings against substituting man-made rites for ones which God has commanded (Matt. 15:3-6; Mark 7:8-13; Col. 2:8; 2 Thess. 2:15; 3:6). [3]

This is no mere stylistic difference in practice, but the reflection of a profoundly different understanding of the nature of baptism and the place of children in the church. We have reserved a full discussion of the meaning and purpose of baptism for a later chapter, but suffice it to say that 'baby dedications' are no substitute for the God-ordained sacrament of baptism. They are not a 'means of grace' whereby God makes certain promises and extends blessings to those upon whom it is bestowed. They do not mark the subject child off from the rest of the unbelieving world and induct him into the membership of Christ's church. They do not involve the use of water to symbolize the cleansing from sin

---

[3] Many Baptists argue that the warrant for baby dedications is found at Luke 2:22-24, where Jesus was presented in the Temple by His parents. But that presentation was in fulfillment of the Old Testament command to present "every firstborn male" child, and involved offering a sacrifice in his place in remembrance of the Lord's sparing of the Israelite children at the Exodus. Moreover, this was also done to accomplish Mary's ceremonial "purification according to the law of Moses" (Luke 2:22). Both of these aspects of Jesus' dedication to the Lord at the Temple were a part of the Old Testament sacrificial system, which was fulfilled in His ultimate sacrifice on the Cross. As a result, modern baby dedications bear no resemblance at all to this Old Testament custom (for good reason!). Johnson, 13-14.

that baptism is meant to represent. And they do not recall the death and resurrection of Christ, and thus do not serve as a sign and seal of the righteousness which we have by faith in Him. In short, baby dedications neither serve the same function, nor have the same divine character and origin, as infant baptism.

Ultimately, the debate concerning infant baptism involves the issue of the place of children in the church. And it is likely that the way in which one views these 'blessing' passages will influence the way in which that ultimate question is resolved (or vice versa). Will we relegate Jesus' words and actions here solely to the realm of sweet expressions of sentiment from a loving Creator towards the most vulnerable of His creatures, or will we acknowledge the spiritual nature and significance of them as well?

When we get to chapter six we will see that the early church not only understood the spiritual significance of these passages, but used them as *direct* support for the practice of infant baptism. One New Testament scholar has even argued that Jesus' injunction to His disciples that they were not to "forbid" the children from coming to Him may have provided the basis for the original baptismal formula of the apostolic church, the traces of which are evident in a number of texts. Thus, as candidates for baptism were brought before the church, the question was posed as to whether or not there was anything which *forbade* or *hindered* the person from receiving baptism (Acts 8:36; 10:47; 11:17; Matt. 3:13-15).[4]

William Hendriksen commented on the first passage above (from its parallel at Matthew 19:13-15) as follows:

> The fact that the Lord regarded these little ones as being already "in" the kingdom, as being even now members of his church, must not escape our attention. He definitely did not view them as "little heathen," who were living outside of the realm of salvation until by an act of their own they would "join the church." He regarded them as "holy seed" (see 1 Cor. 7:14). It must be borne in mind

---

[4] Oscar Cullman, *Baptism in the New Testament*, trans. J.K.S. Reid (London: SCM Press, 1969), 71-80.

that those who brought their little ones to Jesus must have had faith in him... We do not receive the impression that these infants were sick or dying. Yet they were brought to Jesus that he might bless them. This he did, in line with all the assurances of divine favor for believers *and their seed* (Gen. 17:7, 12; Ps. 103:17; 105:6-10; Isa. 59:21; Acts 2:38, 39, to mention only a few)...

The objection might be advanced, "How was it possible for Jesus to say even now that these sucklings were already citizens of his kingdom, heirs of salvation? Did he not know that at least some of them might in later years turn their backs upon him? Why this distinctly *positive* approach?" The answer is that ... the Lord as a rule gathers his church from the circle of believing parents and their children. Just as Jesus said many wonderful things about The Twelve (10:29, 30, 40; 19:28, etc.) without always immediately adding, "I exclude Judas," so also it must be understood here (19:13-15) that those little ones who in later years reject the Lord and persist in this unbelief are not saved.[5]

Returning to the theme which is the organizing principle of this book, we must ask those who would exclude little children from the blessings of membership in Christ's church, 'What are the biblical grounds for doing so?,' and 'Where in the New Testament do we find any hint that God has changed the pattern from Old Testament times concerning the inclusion of children in His visible community on earth?' Those who would argue for such a change bear the burden of proof, not those of us who argue for the continuity of God's design to work His redemptive plan through the unit of the family, as He had done for thousands of years prior to the inception of Christian baptism.

The quote from Hendriksen above is instructive. Any way you slice it, reaching a decision on this issue means asking ourselves if we are going to treat our children as 'little heathen,' or if we are going to recognize them for what they are – 'holy seed.'

---

[5] Hendriksen, 721-22.

It is truly a shame that these passages have been so easily dismissed by some in the Reformed camp, who, in an effort to sound accommodating, or perhaps to focus the attention on other more important passages, have been eager to grant that these passages do not prove the doctrine of infant baptism, and simply move on to other elements of the discussion. But as we stated at the outset, the case for infant baptism is a cumulative one, based not upon one or two single passages in Scripture, but upon the totality of the biblical record. And these passages have a great deal to say to us about God's love and care for His covenant children.

It seems to me that the only possible conclusion that one can draw from such evidence is that the fact that Jesus blessed the little children and said that 'of such is the kingdom of God' is unequivocal support *for* infant baptism, not an argument against it. Jesus' words are clear and direct – Let the little children come to Him!

Chapter 5

The Baptisms in Acts

"Jesus only blessed the little children and only adults were baptized in the Book of Acts." It was with those words that the dear lady we introduced in the last chapter dismissed the doctrine of infant baptism and affirmed her belief that only those of sufficient age and mental capacity were entitled to the waters of Christian baptism.

We have already dealt with the first part of this two-pronged indictment of infant baptism. We turn now to the task of dealing with the second part. And once again the issue is one of silence. This time it is the lack of a single explicit reference to the baptism of an infant child in the book of Acts. Naturally, if it can be demonstrated from the descriptions of baptisms that are recorded for us in that book that no children were baptized, then the case for infant baptism would appear to be weakened. After all, it seems reasonable to expect that we would have been given one record of such an activity having taken place as an example to us if the church was to be charged with continuing the practice throughout the generations to come.

But while the logic of that argument may be reasonable enough, we must first ask if it is not based upon a faulty premise. Is it really true that Acts fails to record a single instance of an infant child receiving the rite of Christian baptism? Ultimately, we are compelled to say that the evidence suggests that the answer is 'No.'

Making our case involves taking a closer look at the actual record of baptisms contained in the book of Acts. For starters, each of the baptisms recorded there may be classified as one of three types (in the order of their appearance): (1) group; 2) individual; or 3) household. The separation into these three categories does not obscure the fact that each person baptized in Acts had the sacrament administered to them *individually*. Rather, the reason for this categorization is because this is the way in which Luke, the author of Acts, described the events for us. Those in the group category, for instance, are not mentioned individually by name, but were baptized because they were part of an identifiable group of persons who came to faith in Christ on the same general occasion. They may not, however, have all been baptized in the same ceremony or on the same day.

There are four such group baptisms recorded for us in Acts: 1) the three thousand souls who were baptized in Jerusalem on the day of Pentecost (Acts 2:41); 2) the unnumbered group of men and women who believed Philip's preaching in Samaria (Acts 8:12); 3) those who believed Paul's preaching in Corinth (Acts 18:8); and 4) the disciples of John the Baptist who had not yet received Christian baptism (Acts 19:5).

Accounts of individual baptisms are no more numerous than the group baptisms mentioned above. The four in this category include: 1) the Ethiopian Eunuch (Acts 8:38); 2) Simon the Sorcerer, one of those baptized in Samaria but mentioned individually (Acts 8:13); 3) the apostle Paul (Acts 9:18); and 4) Gaius, who is only mentioned by name at 1 Cor. 1:14, but appears to have been one of those baptized by Paul in Corinth (Acts 18:8).

What are we able to say about the accounts included in these first two categories of baptisms? The general impression is one of adults being baptized upon their professions of faith in Christ. Indeed, that is certainly the case in all four of the individual accounts and most likely so in at least one of the group accounts (John's disciples). But this is hardly surprising, given that these accounts are merely descriptive of what was taking place as the gospel was being preached in new locales and people were coming to faith. It is what we would expect to see happen as the apostles fulfilled Christ's Great Commission, which included the command to baptize those who became His disciples.

Since prior to the events recounted in the book of Acts no one had as yet received Christian baptism, all of those adults who came to faith through the preaching of the apostles received the sacrament as a sign of their initiation into the new Christian community. Of course, this is the exact same practice that has always been operative in Reformed churches – those who have never received the sign of baptism and come to faith in Christ are baptized in the name of the Father, Son, and Holy Spirit, signifying their union with Christ and membership in the local church.

But beyond this statement of general impression we are able to say almost nothing else about these baptism accounts. In none of the cases are we told anything about the families of those receiving baptism; whether or not they were present at the preaching of the Word or the administration of the baptisms; or whether or not they are to be assumed as part of those to whom reference is made as having received baptism. In at least two of the four cases of individual baptism we know for certain that none of the baptized person's family members (if they even had any) were present at their baptism, and in the others that fact is implied.

As for the group cases, we are merely told that "many believed" and were baptized (18:8), or that three thousand "souls" were added to the church (2:41), or that "both men and women were baptized" (8:12). Even this last reference does nothing to strengthen the case of those who argue for adult baptism only, since the Bible frequently refers to groups of people with terms that are not intended to be understood as exclusive of others. We have no more warrant for assuming that only adults were included in these descriptions than we do for assuming that no Israelite women came out of the captivity in Egypt because Exodus 12:37 makes reference only to "six hundred thousand men on foot, besides children."

In short, there isn't a shred of evidence in the book of Acts that a family member of any person baptized in either of these sets of baptisms was excluded because of their inability to profess faith in Christ on their own.

But if the Baptist claim that only adults were baptized in Acts is merely unsupportable by appealing to the first two categories of baptismal accounts, I believe it to be especially hard to maintain in light of the accounts in the third category, to which we will now turn our attention.

Household Baptisms

It may come as a surprise to many readers to learn that, of the three categories of baptisms we have identified, that of household baptisms is the one which garners the most references in the New Testament. It is possible to identify five separate references to the baptisms of entire households there, with four appearing in the book of Acts, and the fifth to be found in First Corinthians, where a reference is made back to events which took place in the eighteenth chapter of Acts.

The first instance occurs in the familiar story of the conversion of the Roman centurion Cornelius in Acts 10. We are told in verse 24 that Cornelius had gathered his relatives and close friends together in anticipation of Peter's visit to give him "the words by which you and all your household will be saved" (11:14). While Peter was speaking such words to Cornelius and his household "the Holy Spirit fell upon all those who heard the word" (v. 44), and they were immediately baptized in the name of the Lord (v. 48).

The next two references appear in the sixteenth chapter of Acts. In verses 11-15 we read about how the Lord opened the heart of

Lydia to believe Paul's preaching of the gospel, and that she and her household were then baptized as a result. A few verses later is the account of the Philippian jailer who asked Paul and Silas what he must do to be saved. Verses 31-35 record the apostles' answer and then provide important additional details as follows:

> So they said, "Believe on the Lord Jesus Christ, and you will be saved, you and your household." Then they spoke the word of the Lord to him and to all who were in his house. And he took them the same hour of the night and washed their stripes. And immediately he and all his family were baptized. Now when he had brought them into his house, he set food before them; and he rejoiced, having believed in God with all his household.

In a moment we will look more closely at the baptismal accounts of Lydia and the Philippian jailer. But there are two more cases of household baptism that we have not yet mentioned. Acts 18:8 tells us that a man named Crispus, who was the ruler of the synagogue in Corinth, "believed on the Lord with all his household." Then, in 1 Cor. 1:14, Paul informs us that he had personally baptized Crispus. While the text there does not add the detail that the entire household of Crispus was baptized, that fact may reasonably be inferred, both on the basis of the reference to the household in Acts 18:8, as well as from the surrounding context of the First Corinthians passage, where our fifth and final reference is to Paul's baptism of the "household of Stephanus."

What is important to recognize here is that the Jewish understanding of 'household,' to which Paul and the other apostles would have adhered, included all dependent members who resided in the home. This would include not only a person's spouse, but any and all children, and even servants and soldiers who might be quartered in the home. All of these were considered to be a part of one's household. Yet in each of these five cases the reference is to a household being baptized, despite the fact that no other persons are mentioned by name or noted as having also believed. Rather, reference is made only to the faith of the household head (we are left to presume that Lydia was the head of her household).

Understandably, some Baptists have recognized the problem these passages present for the doctrine of believers' baptism. Delos Miles, in his book *How Jesus Won Persons*, admitted this much when he wrote:

> I confess that for a long time I neglected these New Testament references to the salvation of households. Perhaps I was afraid that they might contradict what I believed about believers' baptism by immersion. Subconsciously I am sure that I thought those who practiced infant baptism used such passages to buttress their arguments. So I just steered clear of them.[1]

What Miles and others do in an attempt to mitigate the force of these passages is hinted at in the first sentence of his quote above, where he refers to these accounts not as household baptisms, but as *household salvations*. In effect he has let his theological presupposition (that only believers are to receive baptism) determine his interpretation of the household baptism texts, even though that interpretation is not warranted by the texts themselves.

This tendency on the part of our Baptist brethren was driven home to me some years ago when the very same Pastor who told me that infant baptism was an argument from silence stated from the pulpit that the baptism of Lydia's household took place only because each and every member of her household believed the gospel and was saved! But the text of Acts 16 says nothing of the sort. The text there says very explicitly that the Lord "opened *her* heart" to believe the gospel, and not a word about any others in the household doing the same. Of course, since we know nothing about the age and makeup of the individual members of Lydia's household, it is possible that each and every one of them did indeed place their trust in Christ that day. But it is not possible

---

[1] Delos Miles, *How Jesus Won Persons* (Nashville: Broadman, 1982), 71-72.

to make such an argument from the passage itself without first imposing a believers' baptist theological construct upon it.

All of which leads me to ask if what we are witnessing in this case is anything less than a textbook example of an argument from silence? I doubt that I need not to point out the great irony in all of this.

For further elaboration on this point the case of the Philippian jailer is particularly instructive. This may be surprising since the passage seems at first glance to support the notion that this man's entire household believed the gospel. Luke, the author of Acts, reports on the incident with these words, "and he rejoiced, having believed in God with all his household" (16:34). The difficulty here is that the force of the passage is lost in many of our modern translations, since Luke makes it clear that while *all* of the jailer's household was baptized (v. 33), it is only the jailer himself who is described as rejoicing and believing in the gospel. The use of the singular verb in verse 34 ("he rejoiced") and the singular pronoun in the jailer's original question to the apostles ("what must *I* do to be saved?") pose a serious problem for those who argue for the Baptist understanding of these passages. As Bryan Chapell wrote in his excellent essay on this subject, "the assumption that everyone in those households must have made a faith commitment does not take notice of the careful distinction that Luke makes between those who actually believed and those who were baptized."[2]

Of course, the more practical question that must be raised in this context is whether it makes any sense to assume that *all* of those who were members of each of these five households would have been old enough to make an intelligent profession of faith in Christ. Given the fact that the New Testament was written in an age when families (and particularly *households*) tended to be larger than they are today, what are the odds that not a single child of tender years was to be found in any one of the five households under consideration? Frankly, it seems unreasonable to make such an assumption.

---

[2] Bryan Chapell, "A Pastoral View of Infant Baptism," *The Case for Covenantal Infant Baptism*, 21.

But apart from the issues of whether or not our Baptist friends have imposed their own theological presumptions upon these texts, or have missed the obvious difficulty of assuming that all persons in such households were old enough to rule out child baptism, we find ourselves in the position of having to assert that they are once again guilty of missing the forest for the trees. Because whether or not we are able to prove the existence of young children in the households baptized in Acts, these passages glaringly demonstrate the basic principle that we have contended for from the outset – that God continues in the new covenant era the pattern which He established from the very beginning of history. That pattern involves working out His plan of redemption, in the first instance, through the most basic of human institutions – the family.

Family Solidarity in the Old and New Testaments

The unity and solidarity of the family in the Old Testament record is a fact which no serious student of Scripture would dare to dispute. Over and over again we see this principle in action with respect to God's dealings with individual families. And we see it operative in the realms of both blessing and cursing.

Though it is possible to come up with dozens of examples, the recitation of a few of the more obvious ones proves the point sufficiently for our discussion:

1) Noah – Described as a man who "walked with God," Noah was chosen by Him to build the ark prior to the Great Flood. That flood destroyed all living things except those which Noah had loaded into the ark prior to the rains beginning. This included Noah's "household," as per God's express instructions (Gen. 7:1), which was comprised of Noah's wife, their three sons, and their sons' wives. Thus, an additional seven family members, Noah's entire household, were saved on account of his actions (1 Pet. 3:20). Moreover, Noah's sons were subsequently blessed by God along with him, and received the privilege of being participants in the covenant God made with their father (Gen. 9:8).

2) Abraham – The life of the great Patriarch may be considered the prototype for the family solidarity of which we contend here. Not only do we find in his story the divinely-instituted basis for administering the Old Testament covenant sign to one's household, but he is also the one through whose family lineage the promises descend to future generations. That promise further stated that in him "all the families of the earth shall be blessed" (Gen. 12:3). Admittedly, the meaning and significance of this latter statement go far beyond the bounds of mere physical relationship and descent, but it points to the even more wonderful truth that believers in Christ are "sons of the family of Abraham" (Acts 13:26).

3) The Passover Celebration – Although all of the Israelites were saved from the destruction that God visited upon the Egyptians just prior to the Exodus, Moses told the Israelite adults that when their children inquired of them what it was the Passover meal was meant to symbolize, that they should answer that it was a reminder of how God had delivered their "households" (Ex. 12:27). Since the covenantal status of a household depended upon the faith of the father, each and every Israelite firstborn son that was spared in the Passover event could trace his blessing back to that status which he enjoyed as the circumcised child of an Israelite father.

4) The Destruction of Jericho – In the story of the destruction of Jericho by the Israelites, we see the principle of family solidarity exhibited in both blessing and cursing. In the first instance, God gave explicit instructions to the Israelites to spare Rahab the harlot and her entire household because of her actions in hiding the spies who had been sent into the city beforehand (Josh. 6:17, 25). On the other hand, when a man named Achan kept for himself certain possessions captured in Jericho, the Israelites were commanded by God to burn to death him and his entire family (Josh. 7:15, 24-25).

5) Job – In his conversation with the Lord, Satan recognized that God had placed a hedge around Job's entire household on account of his faith (Job 1:9-10).

6) Adam – Last, but not least, is the example of Adam. As the first created human being and the one with whom God made the original covenant of works, it was Adam's transgression into sin and fall from grace that cast his entire family (the human race) out of the Garden and brought physical and spiritual death into the world. The Westminster Confession of Faith (6:3) says: "They [Adam and Eve] being the root of all mankind, the guilt of this sin was imputed; and the same death in sin, and corrupted nature, conveyed to all their posterity descending from them by ordinary generation." Thus, the actions of one single man resulted in the condemnation of the entire human race (Rom. 5:18). Thankfully, however, that is not the end of the story.

Many more examples of this solidarity could be adduced from Scripture, but we trust that the case has been sufficiently established from those just mentioned. The emphatic point is that the family was viewed by God as a unit, and not as a collection of isolated individuals. Moreover, it was the father (or head of the household) who represented the family in religious matters. The faith of the father was the decisive factor in determining the status of the home as either Israelite or pagan.[3]

But it is precisely this *principle of representation* which we find so difficult to accept in our modern individualistic culture. To the modern mind it is simply inconceivable that anyone else, even one's own father, could determine one's individual status before God or man, even though we would have to admit that our modern law recognizes this very fact in a myriad of ways. Of course, this mindset is particularly entrenched with respect to matters of religion, where the mantra of personal choice is the watchword of the day.

The only question that concerns us here, however, is whether or not the principles of representation and family solidarity carried over into the New Testament dispensation. Did the apostles understand and apply such principles when conducting

[3] Joachim Jeremias, *Infant Baptism in the First Four Centuries*, trans. David Cairns (Eugene, OR: Wipf & Stock, 2004), 22-23.

their missionary efforts in the first decades of building the primitive New Testament church? And is there evidence in the New Testament that this is the case?

Though there is less material with which to work in the New Testament to establish the point, we nevertheless believe that the evidence is more than sufficient to demonstrate the continuing validity of the solidarity principle in matters relating to the Christian life and practice, especially the rite of baptism.

The following evidence is offered in support of this continuing validity:

1) The Use of the House/Household Formula – It may seem as if we are being redundant or circular in our reasoning here by mentioning the use of the household formula to support our case. But in our discussion above we offered such evidence as it related to the baptism of households for the purpose of arguing that the book of Acts included accounts of infant or child baptism. Here we shift the focus ever so slightly by offering such evidence for the purpose of proving that the solidarity principle is alive and well in the New Testament. While this is another way of arguing our case for infant baptism with the same body of evidence, it places that evidence on a firmer footing by rendering as moot the issue of whether there were young children in any of the homes mentioned in Acts (i.e., it focuses on the 'forest' rather than the 'trees').

What is so significant about the use of the terms *house* or *household* in the New Testament is that they already had an established biblical usage. Not only were these terms adopted from the Old Testament cultic language, and particularly the language of circumcision (Gen. 17), but such references were very clear in their implications with respect to the children of the house.[4] Joachim Jeremias wrote in this regard:

The picture is always the same. The phrase 'he and his (whole) house' denotes the complete family; normally

---

[4] Ibid., 21.

husband, wife and children. In no single case is the term 'house' restricted to the adult members of the house, though on the other hand children alone may be mentioned when the whole house is meant. Whilst the slaves are very often not reckoned as part of the 'house,' the inclusion of the children is taken for granted. Indeed, the Old Testament repeatedly lays special emphasis on the very smallest being reckoned in.[5]

Jeremias goes on to point out that since the primitive church took over this phrase in its firmly established form, it is only reasonable to assume that its usage in the New Testament is meant to convey the same sense of meaning. It was the principle of household solidarity that formed the basis for infant circumcision, and there is no indication anywhere in the New Testament record that the apostles and early church missionaries understood the arrangement in the post-Pentecost era to be any different from what had applied for two thousand years. The household was a recognized group of persons united under the headship of the father, whose religious convictions determined the status of the house before God.

This state of affairs is represented perfectly by the exchange between the Philippian jailer and the apostles that we looked at earlier. When the jailer asked the question, "Sirs, what must *I* do to be saved?" the apostles answered back, "Believe on the Lord Jesus Christ, and you will be saved, *you and your household*" (Acts 16:30-31). The jailer did not ask how it was that his household could be saved, nor did he need to. But the apostles' answer confirms for us that the representative principle that defined such family relationships in the Old Testament era is alive and well in the New. The fact that the apostles and authors of the New Testament intentionally used terms so closely associated with circumcision in their description of baptisms is powerful evidence that they understood the latter to be a replacement

---

[5] Joachim Jeremias, *The Origins of Infant Baptism: A Further Study in Reply to Kurt Aland*, trans. Dorothea M. Barton (Eugene, OR: Wipf & Stock, 2004), 24.

for the former, and that they further applied it on the same basis as the former.

2) Acts 2:38-39 – Peter's words on the day of Pentecost that the promise was to "you and to your children" only make sense in light of the earlier promises given to the Jewish people, promises that always embraced their offspring. According to Murray, this "demonstrates that Peter, in the illumination and power of the Spirit of Pentecost, recognised that there was no suspension or abrogation of that divine administration whereby children are embraced with their parents in God's covenant promise."[6]

3) 1 Cor. 7:14 – The fact that the child of a believer in Christ is considered "holy" is proof positive that the representative principle of the Old Testament period lives on unabated in the New.

4) 1 Cor. 10:1-11 – In an interesting take on the biblical story, Paul describes the Israelites' passage through the Red Sea (on dry land) as a baptism into Moses. Why else would Paul use that phrase to describe an event which included in its scope every man, woman, and child of the nation if he had understood baptism to be reserved for adult believers only?

5) Jesus Christ – Just as we concluded our list of Old Testament examples with Adam, so must we finish now with the Second Adam, Jesus Christ. Jesus is the representative head of all those who place their trust in Him, removing the curse of the law that the first Adam had earned for every one of us (Rom. 5:17-19). Trusting in Christ makes one a member of the "household of God" (Eph. 2:19). Although this "family" is not one based on bloodline or descent, it is a family nonetheless. And membership in it is based upon Jesus' work being credited to one's account, which in turn is based upon God's good pleasure alone. For those who decry the principle of representative headship, this is the ultimate obstacle to a rational and consistent understanding of the redemptive work of Christ.

As we conclude our study of the baptisms in Acts, it is helpful to point out just how few instances of baptism are actually recorded

---

[6] Murray, 68.

for us in the New Testament. The fact that five of the thirteen recorded baptisms are baptisms of entire households makes their significance all the more obvious. Since we know that there must have been thousands of individual baptisms during the years covered by the book of Acts, we may also reasonably presume that there were thousands of household baptisms during that period as well. The book of Acts is not an exhaustive account of the work of the apostles in the years between 30 and 60 AD. Rather, it merely shows us the *pattern* for the way in which the gospel was proclaimed and administered, first in Jerusalem, then in Judea and Samaria, and finally to the ends of the earth (Acts 1:8).

What many Christians seem to overlook when they read their Bibles is that the New Testament (and particularly the book of Acts) was written in this missionary context. The baptisms that are recorded for us are missionary baptisms; that is, they show baptism being administered to adult converts coming into the church from both Jewish and Gentile backgrounds, none of whom had yet received the sign of the new covenant. Hence, if the solidarity of the family that was an established principle of the Old Testament church is assumed, then it makes perfect sense that neither Luke, nor any of the other biblical writers, would feel the need to emphasize the baptism of children, nor seek to justify the practice. As Jeremias wrote, children were "hidden in the bosom of the family," and were not the center of attention in these missionary-specific accounts.[7]

What is instructive to note is that in every single instance in the New Testament where a person is identified as having a household present at his or her conversion the household was also baptized.[8] For this reason, William Shishko remarks that, "The point is not that infants were baptized in the New Testament, but that *whole households* were baptized." He further adds that:

> *All* of God's covenants have included families. Even the major prophecies of the new covenant clearly indicate

---

[7] Jeremias, *Infant Baptism in the First Four Centuries*, 19, 23.
[8] Chapell, 19.

the continuance of the household as the basic unit of the people of God. See Gen. 12:3; Isa. 54:10, 13; 59:21 (the Old Testament backdrop to Acts 2:39); 61:8-9; Jer. 32:38-40; Ezek. 37:25-26; Zech. 8:5; 10:7, 9: 12:10-14; 14:17 ... If noble Christians "searched the Scriptures" (i.e., the Old Testament) to find out whether the things taught by the apostles were so (Acts 17:11), where would they have found warrant to abrogate the household principle?[9]

Shishko's question provides a fitting conclusion to our discussion of the baptismal accounts in the book of Acts. As his comments point out, we are once again confronted with a certain silence regarding these matters. But the silence concerns the lack of authorization for abrogating a principle that was not only firmly entrenched within the religious understanding and practice of God's people, but was established in the first place by His clear and direct command.

---

[9] Shishko, 7.

Chapter 6

The Evidence from Church History

We turn now to the evidence for the practice of infant baptism which is available to us through a look at the historical records of the church in the first several hundred years after the death of Christ. This includes the period during which the New Testament was being written down for our benefit, and continues through the end of the fourth century. Though we cannot offer an exhaustive treatment of the evidence in so short a work as this, what we do offer is nevertheless an important part of the case for paedobaptism, since, as we shall see, it does much to confirm and support the biblical case that we have made thus far.

The historical evidence comes in several forms, though it consists mainly of the testimony of the early church fathers as to the practice of the church in various locales and time periods. Because it is easy to detect certain changes in thought taking place throughout the time period under review, we take a chronological approach to this patristic evidence so that this development of thought surrounding the issue of baptism may be brought to light.

Some of the evidence is indirect and merely inferential, while some is of a more direct nature and is, in many cases, incontrovertible in demonstrating the historical practice of the early church at specific points in time. Both types of evidence are valuable, however, and taken as a whole help to place the argument for infant baptism on a firm historical footing. Though historical evidence must never be allowed to supplant the clear teaching of Scripture, the evidence from church history helps to establish how the early church, which stood much closer in time to the apostles than do we, understood and applied the injunction to baptize the nations. By looking at the evidence from history, then, it is hoped that we may be able to confirm the *biblical* practice of baptism as it was handed down by Christ and His apostles.

The Evidence from the Apostolic Period (First Century)

Although we have looked in-depth at the biblical evidence and laid out our positive case for the practice of infant baptism, there are several more observations to be made with respect to the New Testament record. Here again we are in the position of noting a peculiar silence; a silence which strengthens the case that we have already put forth. As with the issue of a change in the status of children in the new covenant, it is the lack of evidence in certain matters that grabs our attention here.

Baptist Christians are fond of asking their Reformed brethren to produce a single passage in the New Testament where we see a young child receiving baptism. The five chapters up to this point have been our response to that basic query. But if it is reasonable to ask such a question (which we acknowledge that it is), the same line of questioning may be turned toward the believer's baptism argument. And when we shine the light of the New Testament upon that argument, a number of glaring deficiencies begin to surface (in addition to the ones we have already discussed).

In this regard, we pose the following three questions to those who argue that believer's-only baptism was the New Testament model:

1) Where is the historical evidence from the New Testament that Christ and the apostles instituted a new practice with respect to the inclusion of children in the church?

This may sound like the same question that we posed at the end of chapter three, but there we asked the question primarily with respect to the *prescriptive textual* evidence for such a change. That is, we asked the Baptist to show us where in the New Testament we might find positive biblical injunction for excluding the children of believers from receiving the sign of the covenant. Here our focus is upon the *historical* evidence as we see it in the New Testament, primarily Acts. And the question is posed for one very simple reason – if a change of such magnitude had been implemented by the apostles, we would expect to see some record in the New Testament of Jewish resistance to such a change.

In this context, we are immediately reminded of the New Testament witness to the following: a) Jewish resistance to Jesus' teaching on the Sabbath; b) Jewish resistance to Jesus' attitude toward the purification rites of the Old Testament; c) the disapproval that Jesus encountered when He was seen as skirting various social barriers and customs of first century Judaism (e.g., personally addressing women with whom He was not acquainted, eating with 'sinners,' and relating to the Roman authorities); d) Peter and the other apostles' initial resistance to the inclusion of Gentiles on an equal footing with Jews; and e) Jewish resistance to the apostles' injunctions against circumcision as a requirement for becoming a Christian.

In each of these accounts (and more left unmentioned) the New Testament writers have left us the historical record of a controversy arising from Jewish opposition to a change in practice (whether real or perceived) which was precipitated by the coming of Christ and the inauguration of the new covenant era. But where, we ask, is the outcry over this supposed new arrangement whereby the children of believers were no longer to be marked out as God's special possessions? The New Testament is devoid of even a hint that an objection was raised against the practice at any point in time. But is it realistic to imagine that the church would undertake such a radical shift in ecclesiology and say nothing about it in the process?

The Jews who battled with Paul throughout the book of Acts were continually looking for ways to undermine his authority and assert that he was urging upon the people of God strange new doctrines, in order to demonstrate that he was not one of them. Acts 21:21 proves that they were relentless in their efforts to brand Paul as anti-Jewish for his teaching regarding the administration of circumcision. What better way to take the argument to new heights than by throwing in this additional example of heresy (if it existed)? Yet we hear not a word uttered against Paul in this regard.

2) Where is the historical evidence that the church began, either in the apostolic period or sometime afterwards, to maintain separate rolls for those who had received Christian baptism and those who had not (e.g., their children)? Furthermore, where is the historical evidence for the practice of 'baby dedications'?

If the original practice of the church had been based on the believer's baptism model, then it is surprising that we find no evidence that the children of believers were not in some way accounted for separately from those old enough to profess faith and receive baptism. Of course, most modern Baptists would simply respond that because children are not members of the church they do not belong on the church's rolls in the first place. Fair enough, but what about separate rolls for those who had been the subject of 'baby dedications'? More to the point, where is the evidence that the early church even adhered to such a practice? The fact is that there is no evidence for such a practice in either the historical accounts or the surviving baptismal liturgies. And this is true for both the apostolic period as well as the centuries that followed.

Raising the question of dual membership rolls is not a desperate attempt to throw out any and all possible arguments against the doctrine of believer's baptism. There are some

Reformed churches that keep separate rolls, delineating between "baptized covenant children" and "non-baptized covenant children." There are even a few churches out there that perform both infant baptisms and baby dedications. But neither separate rolls nor baby dedications find support from the records of the primitive church. In the end, the absence of any evidence that the early church treated the children of believers any differently than they had been treated in the Old Testament period, as living within the bosom of the family, makes the Baptist case against infant baptism less tenable.

3) Where in the New Testament is the historical evidence for even a single case of an adult who had grown up in a Christian home receiving baptism upon profession of faith?

If the last issue makes the Baptist case less tenable, this one leaves it with a gaping hole! Despite the fact that the book of Acts covers a thirty year period, more than enough time for the next generation of believers to grow up and make their own professions of faith and be baptized, there isn't a single account in its twenty-eight chapters of such an event taking place. Undoubtedly, there would have been thousands of such examples available for Luke to report on, if believer's baptism had actually been the custom of the early church. But the record is, once again, strangely silent.

In my view, this is one of the most damaging omissions of the biblical/historical record with which a Baptist Christian must contend. Oscar Cullman recognized as much when he wrote:

> Those who dispute the Biblical character of infant baptism have therefore to reckon with the fact that *adult baptism for sons and daughters born of Christian parents, which they recommend, is even worse attested by the New Testament than infant baptism* (for which certain possible traces are discoverable) *and indeed lacks any kind of proof.*[1]

---

[1] Cullman, *Baptism in the New Testament*, 26.

But in addition to the questions we have raised, there is one additional piece of evidence from the first century that is relevant to our discussion here – and that is the practice of proselyte baptism. While much ink has been spilled over the origins of the practice and its precise dating, it is now more-or-less taken for granted that the practice predates that of Christian baptism.[2] And whereas it had earlier been sufficient for Gentile converts to receive circumcision as the rite of entry into the Old Testament church, somewhere in the first century BC Jews began to regard Gentiles as impure and to require the additional step of being baptized.[3]

In his book *Infant Baptism in the First Four Centuries*, Professor Jeremias discussed the similarities between proselyte baptism and Christian baptism. He noted that there were not merely individual points of contact between the two, "but that the whole terminology of the Jewish conversion theology connected with proselyte baptism recurs in the theology of primitive Christian baptism."[4] Thus, he writes, "the only possible conclusion is that the rites are related as parent and child."[5]

Given this reality, then, it is instructive that "the oldest rabbinic sources take it completely for granted that the children, even the smallest children, were admitted with their parents into the Jewish faith," and would not only have been baptized, but in the case of boys, would have been circumcised as well.[6] This fact, coupled with Paul's assertion that baptism was the 'circumcision of Christ,' makes it highly probable that the ritual features and practices of proselyte baptism (and, in this context, circumcision) were carried over into its Christian counterpart, thereby encompassing the entire 'household' within its administration.[7]

---

[2] Everett Ferguson, *Backgrounds of Early Christianity*, 2nd ed. (Grand Rapids: Eerdmans, 1993), 513.

[3] Jeremias, *Infant Baptism in the First Four Centuries*, 25-26.

[4] Ibid., 36.

[5] Ibid.

[6] Ibid., 39.

[7] Ibid., 39-40. Jeremias' comments in this regard are particularly forceful given the progression in his own thinking over time. In the original German edition of his work he had argued that it was quite possible that Christian parents in Corinth, on the

The Evidence from the Post-Apostolic Period (Second Century)

As we move into the post-apostolic period (the second century), we will notice that there is very little direct evidence regarding the baptismal practice of the church that comes from the period itself. Original Christian writings are still relatively scarce during this period, and what little sources do exist are concerned primarily with matters of defending Christianity against various charges brought by her enemies. It is not until the third century that the sources become much more plentiful, and references to baptism become more direct. More importantly, some of those references take us back in time into the period under consideration here.

Nevertheless, there are a handful of writings from the second century which seem to confirm the point for which we contend; even if advocates of believer's baptism would dispute with the inferences we draw from such writings. We will look at the more indirect references first and then move on to the two from this period that are most valuable for our purposes.

Three of the references are of the same general nature and consist of statements which imply the baptism of particular individuals at very young ages, even if they make no explicit reference to the rite of baptism itself. The first comes from the account given by the church in the ancient city of Smyrna (Asia Minor; modern Turkey), which recorded the martyrdom of their eighty-six year-old bishop, Polycarp. The account

basis of 1 Cor. 7:14, did not baptize the children born *subsequent* to their conversion to Christianity. This was so because proselyte baptism had distinguished between the Gentile children who were already born upon their parents' conversion to the faith and those who were born afterwards. Only the former received baptism, while the latter were considered to be born 'in holiness,' and thus did not require the ritual cleansing that proselyte baptism conferred. By the time Jeremias composed the English edition of his work, however, he had recognized that his earlier assumption had not taken into account the fact that all Jewish boys, whether their birth had been 'in holiness' or not, received circumcision on the eighth day. Paul's assertion that baptism had replaced circumcision, then, rendered it impossible to "preclude the possibility that they were baptized" (p. 47). When his follow-up work *The Origins of Infant Baptism* came along two years later, Jeremias was now willing to use even stronger language: "[T]here is just as much reason, indeed perhaps more reason, for the conclusion that, as Judaism circumcised male infants even when born 'in holiness', so Christians baptized children even when born as 'holy'... After all, the 'sanctification' of the pagan husband or wife did not in any way exclude his or her conversion and baptism" (p. 38).

reports that when Polycarp was commanded to revile Christ, he answered, "For eighty-six years I have served him, and he never did me any wrong. How can I blaspheme my King who saved me?" Since the ancient sources allow us to date this event to probably no later than 167-68 AD, it would mean that Polycarp had been born around the year 80 AD.[8] Because his statement was obviously meant to cover the entirety of his life, it is probable that he had been born of Christian parents, and thus may be an indirect reference to his own baptism as an infant in that time period.[9]

A similar story involves a man named Polycrates, who was bishop of Ephesus in the late second century. In a message he sent to Rome in 190-91 AD he wrote, "I now, my brethren, have lived in the Lord sixty-five years."[10] If we again assume that this is a reference to his own baptism as either an infant or young child, it would place his birth at around 125 AD.

The third of these references comes to us from the pen of Justin Martyr. In his *First Apology*, written around 150-55 AD, he mentions "many men and women of the age of sixty and seventy years who have been disciples of Christ from childhood," and who had kept their Christian faith untarnished throughout all of those years.[11] Jeremias notes that the use of the passive word for 'becoming a Christian' which Justin employed here implies that he was making reference to their baptisms.[12] If so, then we have in Justin's account another indirect reference to infant baptism which carries us all the way back to apostolic times, since the people mentioned by him would have received baptism in the last two decades of the first century, a period when the apostle John was still alive.

A non-Christian source from this time period is a letter written by the historian Pliny the Younger around the year 112.

---

[8] Ibid., 59-62. F.F. Bruce places the date of Polycarp's martyrdom even earlier, at 156 AD. See F.F. Bruce, *The Spreading Flame* (Grand Rapids: Eerdmans, 1995), 174.
[9] Ibid., 63.
[10] Ibid.
[11] Ibid., 72.
[12] Ibid.

In it he speaks of the *very young*, who along with adults belong to the church.[13]

Obviously, none of these four references *proves* that infant baptism was being practiced in the churches of the first or second century. Thus, it is understandable that Baptists have tended to dispute the inferences which we have suggested should be drawn from them. On the other hand, it should be pointed out that the ancient Christians understood the difference between the number of years a person had lived and the number of years one had been a Christian. For those born into Christian homes, however, it would have been common for them to reckon this time period from the date of baptism. Thus, the inference we have drawn from the above accounts is not only a reasonable one, but it is the most natural one.

Furthermore, even if it be true that these references do not prove anything definitively, it is also true that there is no evidence whatsoever from this time period that believer's baptism had become the norm in the church. And we have yet to get to the last two references, which in my view place us on much firmer evidential ground when trying to establish the early church's baptismal practice in the second century.

The first of these two references comes from Aristides of Athens, who wrote an *Apology* for the Christian faith sometime during the reign of Hadrian (117-138 AD). He wrote, "And when a child is born to them *they thank God*; and if it die in infancy, they thank him exceedingly, because it departed this life sinless." Since Aristides always used the expression "to thank God" to describe Christian rites, and in one place in the same document used it specifically to refer to baptism, the context of this statement makes it almost unthinkable that he is not referring to baptism here.[14] This, then, would be a direct confirmation of the practice of infant baptism in Greece from a period only a few decades removed from the apostle John's life.

---

[13] Ibid., 63.
[14] Ibid., 70-71.

The second reference is even more illuminating since it comes from the great church father Irenaeus of Lyons. Around the year 180 AD he wrote, "For he [Jesus] has come to save all of them by himself: all those, I say, who through him are reborn into God, infants, young children, boys, the mature and older people." Since Irenaeus followed the uniform terminology of the church at that time in describing baptism as 'regeneration into God,' his words serve as further confirmation for the practice of infant baptism at this early date.[15] Moreover, Irenaeus' words are given added weight by the fact that he was a disciple of Polycarp, who in turn was a disciple of the apostle John. In a letter to his friend Florinus, who had been his companion at Polycarp's feet, Irenaeus recalled how the great bishop had "reported everything in harmony with the Scriptures, as he had received it from the eyewitnesses of the Word of life."[16]

The Evidence from the Third and Fourth Centuries

Although the material from the third and fourth centuries is further removed in time from the evidence we just covered, it is, for reasons which will become obvious, perhaps even more valuable for determining the baptismal practice of the early church. The two most important writings from this period come from the church fathers Origen and Hippolytus.

Origen was born around 185 AD in Alexandria, Egypt and is considered one of the most influential and learned fathers of the early Eastern church. In three separate writings composed during the years 233 to 251, Origen explicitly mentions infant baptism as the universal custom of the church, adding in one instance that the church had received the tradition directly from the apostles.[17]

There are two reasons why Origen's statements are so valuable. First, he was born into a family which had been Christian for several generations. With his birth occurring around 185, we can safely assume, then, that his grandfather's baptism would

---

[15] Ibid., 72-73.

[16] Bruce, *The Spreading Flame*, 275.

[17] Jeremias, *Infant Baptism in the First Four Centuries*, 65-66.

take us back into the early part of the second century.[18] Second, Origen's testimony is especially valuable because of his wide knowledge of practices throughout the Empire at that time. During his long ministry he visited churches in Palestine, Rome, Greece, Western Syria, Cappadocia, and parts of Arabia. Thus, not only would he have been familiar with the practices in those various locations, but his testimony that it was the practice handed down by the apostles implies that he found no deviations from that norm in his travels.[19]

As important as Origen's testimony is with respect to the practice of the Eastern church, so is the testimony of Hippolytus for the Western half of the Empire. Around the year 215 Hippolytus, an elder in the church at Rome, compiled a guidebook on the practices of the church there which is entitled *The Apostolic Tradition*. As the name implies, the goal of Hippolytus was to enumerate and preserve for history the church traditions which he believed had apostolic warrant, and were presumably practiced in the church at Rome at that time. Indeed, though he compiled his information in 215, the material contained therein is obviously much older, and thus takes us back at least several decades in time.[20] Hippolytus not only affirmed the practice of infant baptism as apostolic in origin and the only practice adhered to in the church at that time, but the liturgical details outlined in his work went on to become the standard reference for a great part of the Western church in the centuries that followed.[21]

The lone voice to utter a word against infant baptism from the early church period was Tertullian, an elder in the church at Carthage who wrote a treatise entitled *On Baptism* around the year 200. However, he did not object to infant baptism on scriptural or traditional grounds, but for purely practical reasons. Tertullian believed that baptizing young children laid too great a responsibility on the godparents or sponsors of those coming into the church from paganism, since they

---

[18] Ibid., 66.
[19] Ibid., 70.
[20] Ibid., 74.
[21] Ibid., 75.

might die and not be able to fulfill their responsibilities to oversee the character and life of those whom they sponsored for membership in the church.[22]

Indeed, his remarks make it clear that he did not object to the baptism of the children of Christian parents, but only those coming into the church from paganism, since it was only they who needed sponsors for their baptism. Like the rest of his contemporaries, Tertullian acknowledged Matthew 19:14 ("Forbid them not ...") to be an instruction to baptize children, but worried about the youngest receiving it, since he believed that they were not yet in need of the forgiveness which baptism offers.[23]

Most importantly, Tertullian directed his comments toward what he acknowledged was the established practice of the church in his day, and without the slightest hint that he believed it had ever been anything else. Thus, the church historian Philip Schaff wrote: "Among the fathers, Tertullian himself not excepted – for he combats only its expediency – there is not a single voice against the lawfulness and the apostolic origin of infant baptism."[24]

Nor did Tertullian's views have much of an impact even on the church in North Africa at the time. Half a century later, Tertullian's disciple Cyprian presided over a synod of 67 bishops held in Carthage to decide the question, posed by one Bishop Fidus, whether baptism should be administered on the eighth day of life, as was circumcision. The synod voted unanimously against legislating even this brief delay, holding instead that baptism should be administered on the second or third day of life.[25]

For his part, Tertullian later abandoned the orthodox church and joined the Montanists, a heretical sect that flourished in the second and third centuries. But although his views had no real influence at the time, he foreshadowed to some extent the trend which would arise in the fourth century to postpone baptism on the unbiblical basis that post-baptismal sins were

---

[22] Ibid., 81-83.

[23] Ibid., 81.

[24] Philip Schaff, *History of the Christian Church* (Peabody, MA: Hendrickson, 5th ed., 2002), 2.259.

[25] Jeremias, *Infant Baptism in the First Four Centuries*, 85.

unforgivable, thus rendering baptism before the later years or days of life undesirable.[26]

This tendency to postpone baptism erupted full force in the middle of the fourth century, after the Emperor Constantine was converted in the year 312 and Christianity attained fashionable status. As hundreds of thousands of new converts (some genuine and some not so) flocked into the church, they brought many of their formerly pagan superstitions with them. And by virtue of the sheer number of new converts, which strained the fourth century church's resources and organizational ability, certain of those ideas made their way into the practices of the church. One of the practices affected by the new set of ideas was baptism.

The 'mystery religions' which flourished in the Roman Empire during this time were strictly for the spiritually *enlightened ones*, those who lived life in accordance with its principles and adhered to its rituals and beliefs. There was no parallel to baptism in the mystery religions, although initiation was presented as a 'pagan regeneration' in which a rebirth of sorts took place.[27] Everett Ferguson writes: "Whereas Christianity welcomed the unworthy, the pagan mysteries were for those already pure individuals who met accepted social standards ... Initiation was for the inner circle, not for the whole community of worshipers."[28]

To this notion of a spiritual elite membership was added the already developing idea of the magical efficacy of the ritual of baptism. In the mystery religions, the outward rite was highly esteemed and it was understood that no one could benefit from the blessings offered by the religion except through participation in its rituals.[29] In parallel movement, Christianity had been trending for some time toward the twin notions of baptismal regeneration and that outside the church (and its sacraments) there was no possibility of salvation. The changes taking shape in the makeup of the church only hastened this development.

---

[26] Schaff, 261.
[27] Ferguson, 280.
[28] Ibid., 281.
[29] Bruce, *The Spreading Flame*, 207.

Given this confluence of ideas it is no wonder that infant baptism began to have its detractors. If the pagan idea that initiation was for an inner circle who were already purified made headway in the church's thinking and practice during this time, it is no surprise then that infants were not counted among those worthy to receive the rite of initiation and membership in the select group.

Perhaps more influential in the postponement of baptism, however, was the notion that the magical efficacy of the rite made it desirable to delay reception of the sacrament until such a time as it would have maximum effect. Once the rite became associated with the actual remission of sins, and was coupled with the unbiblical notion that post-baptismal sins could not be forgiven, it was only natural that people began to delay their baptisms until the last possible moment before death, if possible, or at least until some moment in time when the trials and temptations of youth had passed.[30] The model for this behavior was Constantine himself, who delayed his own baptism until he was on his deathbed. But it also happened with some frequency in the case of both pagan converts and Christian parents who opted to delay baptizing their own children during this time period.

Thankfully, we have no problem in dating the period for which this tendency was prevalent in the church. While the seeds of this tendency pre-date the conversion of Constantine in 312, it does not appear to have been a widespread practice until after that time, coinciding, as we have already noted, with the influx of new converts into the church subsequent to that event. Furthermore, there is no particular case which may be cited for the practice of Christian parents postponing the baptism of their infant children prior to the year 329/30, when the later-to-be church father Gregory of Nazianzus was born.[31]

Gregory was one of a number of high profile church leaders in the latter half of the fourth century who reported that their own

---

[30] Augustine (born 354) testified to hearing, during the early years of his life, the refrain to "Let him alone, let him do as he pleases, for he is not yet baptized." Jeremias, *Infant Baptism in the First Four Centuries*, 88.

[31] Ibid., 89.

baptisms had been postponed by their Christian parents (the others being Basil the Great, Ambrose, Chrysostom, Jerome, and Augustine). But each of these men was born between the years 329 and 354. So the problem seems to have reached its acute stage during these first few decades after the conversion of the empire to Christianity.[32]

This proposed dating is also supported by the fact that a new phenomenon arose in the middle of the fourth century – tombstone inscriptions which identify the dead persons as neophytes (newly baptized). The title was applied to both children and adults, and occurs only until around the year 400 with any regularity.[33]

In fact, the written evidence is suggestive of a very short period of time during which this crisis played itself out within the church. According to Jeremias, after the year 365 the literary sources begin once more to cite infant baptism as the universal custom of the church, and to justify it theologically, as if nothing at all had happened.[34] Even some of the very same theologians whose baptism had been delayed by their parents were arguing strenuously for the practice of infant baptism by the end of the century.[35] The Pelagian controversy, which arose in the early years of the fifth century, put an end to the crisis once and for all.[36]

Moreover, it would be wrong to infer that even during the fourth century infant baptism had fallen out of general favor, since there is evidence for the maintenance of the practice from three separate sources: 1) the numerous church orders that were based upon Hippolytus' work; 2) the decisions of the Synod of Elvira in Spain (306/312) touching upon the baptism of infants;

---

[32] Ibid., 88-89, 95. It should be noted that this development was *not* a movement toward the practice of believer's baptism, at least not as it is propounded by modern Baptists; for each of these men waited well into their adult years, long after the inception of their public ministries (and after the temptations of youth had subsided), to undergo baptism. Moreover, 'emergency' baptisms were often administered to those about to die, regardless of their age or ability to profess faith in Christ.

[33] Ibid., 89.

[34] Ibid., 94.

[35] Ibid., 95.

[36] Ibid., 97.

and 3) tombstone inscriptions which testify to the administration of baptism to the infant children of Christian parents throughout this time period.[37] Thus, we are warranted in saying, as Jeremias does, that the custom of infant baptism has "continued *unbroken*" since the inception of the church.[38]

The Baptist Argument from Church History

From the assumed starting point that believer's baptism was the teaching and practice of the apostolic church, we may state the Baptist argument from church history, in its most basic terms, as follows: 1) somewhere between the end of the apostolic era and the year 200 the practice was changed to include the baptism of infants and young children; 2) even after this date the practice was not uniform, as evidenced by the various baptismal liturgies from this time period which give no instructions for the baptism of infants; 3) throughout the third and fourth centuries there was continued resistance to the novelty of infant baptism from certain quarters; and 4) eventually the infant baptism position won out over the established norm of believer's baptism as the church grappled with issues such as infant mortality, original sin, and baptismal regeneration.

This four-part argument is essentially that put forth by Dr. Steven A. McKinion, an associate professor of Historical Theology and Patristic Studies at Southeastern Baptist Theological Seminary. Dr. McKinion contributed an essay entitled "Baptism in the Patristic Writings" in the recently released book *Believer's Baptism: Sign of the New Covenant in Christ*,[39] which is a defense of the Baptist position by some of the most able theologians from that tradition today. In order to understand the Baptist case more fully, we will examine McKinion's arguments on their own terms, as well as in light of the evidence which we have already laid out.

---

[37] Ibid., 91-93.

[38] Ibid., 92.

[39] Steven A. McKinion, "Baptism in the Patristic Writings," *Believer's Baptism: Sign of the New Covenant in Christ*, eds. Thomas R. Schreiner and Shawn D. Wright (Nashville: B&H, 2006).

It is fair to say that the heart of Dr. McKinion's positive case for believer's baptism is the apparent lack of explicit instructions given for the baptism of infants in some of the earliest liturgical writings and manuals for church order which have survived and are available to us. But as we shall see, not only is there far less to this argument than meets the eye, but in several cases McKinion ignores or dismisses evidence from the very same sources which run contrary to his position.

At the outset of his essay, McKinion sets out to address what is an undeniable fact: that infant baptism appears in the patristic writings as a settled practice by the beginning of the third century, without any evidence from the intervening period that a change in practice had taken place. He writes:

> There is no doubt that infant baptism was practiced quite early in the church's history, but the prevalence of the practice, its significance, and its origin are a matter of contention …[D]oes the existence of infant baptism in the third century necessarily mean that the practice is ancient? If the practice began in the third century rather than in apostolic times, one might wonder why there is no fanfare accompanying a change of such magnitude in one of Christianity's most central components. The absence of any debates in the literature of the second century could lead one to conclude that the practice was a tradition received from the apostles rather than an innovation. Despite the appearance of infant baptism in the patristic writings of the third century and beyond, there is no necessary attribution of antiquity to the practice. *One might just as likely conclude that the practice is novel as that it is ancient* [emphasis added].[40]

This is a curious statement. Given McKinion's admission that there is no evidence in the literature of the second century suggesting a change in practice from what the apostles had handed

---

[40] Ibid., 165.

down, how then could it be *just as likely* that such a change had taken place? Wouldn't common sense dictate just the opposite conclusion? At a minimum, the facts of the early witness to infant baptism and the lack of any competing evidence places the burden of proof on those who would label the practice a *novelty*.

A similar, but even more curious statement, appears in McKinion's discussion of Tertullian's *On Baptism*, the treatise from 200 AD that testifies to the established practice of infant baptism in North Africa. In a casual manner, Dr. McKinion remarks that Tertullian wrote his treatise "in response to the innovative practice of infant baptism."[41] Of course, such a statement fits perfectly with McKinion's presupposition that believer's baptism was the apostolic model. But there is just one little problem with such a statement: there isn't a shred of evidence in Tertullian's treatise that suggests he considered infant baptism to be an innovation! On the contrary, as historian Philip Schaff noted, "He meets it not as an innovation, but as a prevalent custom."[42]

Rather than testifying to an innovation in practice, it was Tertullian who urged an innovation upon the church of his day. He was the first of those who would become more prevalent in the fourth century, even if for different reasons, who sought to push the church away from the practice of baptizing children until a certain age limit had been reached. Recall that it was Tertullian who testified to the use of Matthew 19:14 as support for the biblical call to baptize infants in the first place, though he was beginning to have his doubts about the wisdom of such an injunction. Perhaps, then, it is not surprising that it was only a few years later that he left the orthodox church for the Montanist sect, as his views became less and less moored to the teachings of Scripture.

When McKinion addresses the patristic references to particular believers having lived their entire lives as followers of Christ, such as those from Polycarp, Polycrates, and Justin Martyr, he dismisses them as nothing more than attempts "to highlight a believer's

---

[41] Ibid., 173.
[42] Schaff, 261.

faithful devotion to Christ from 'youth.'" Then he continues, "It is just as likely that the martyr, or other believer, was baptized as a young child, or even an older child, as it is that he or she was baptized as an infant."[43] Even while admitting of the possibility, we must once again ask, is it really *just as likely*? As evidence for his position, Dr. McKinion offers the following personal note:

> Anecdotally, for many years my own description of my conversion (or testimony) began, "I was raised in a Christian home." Someone writing of my view of baptism a hundred years from now would be mistaken to conclude either that I was baptized as an infant or that I believed in household baptisms. A lifelong Baptist, I was baptized as a twelve-year-old believer, and have never intended by my earlier statement to imply that I was a Christian prior to my conversion.[44]

But McKinion's anecdote begs the question: if he found himself, like Polycarp, as an eighty-six year-old about to face martyrdom, would he say of himself that he had served Christ for eighty-six years, as did the aged bishop? Or would he answer that he had served Him for seventy-four years? His statement above clearly implies the latter. There is no reason to presume that Polycarp and the early Christians understood things any differently. Like McKinion, it is probable that they dated the length of their Christian service from the time of their baptism.

Most of the remainder of McKinion's case centers on the instructions for baptism given in a number of church writings from the first few centuries. The first two sources he cites are the *Didache*, a second century church manual which included details related to administering the rite of baptism, and Justin Martyr's *First Apology*, which we discussed above. Both are offered for the same basic reason: in their discussions of who is to receive baptism, and the requirements that are placed upon such

---

[43] McKinion, 172.
[44] Ibid., 172-73.

candidates, they seem to imply that baptism is reserved for adults and older children. For example, both of these works instruct the candidate for baptism to fast for one or two days beforehand, and Justin's *Apology* also describes such candidates as those who have repented of their sins.[45] From these instructions it is argued that there is no place for children at the baptismal font, since they are incapable of either fasting or repenting.

But the fact that a few early church writings contain language directed toward adults, with nothing specific regarding the procedure for baptizing infants, is hardly surprising, given the scriptural basis of their instructions; nor is it proof of anything other than that, as we have already argued, the children of believers were hidden "within the bosom of the family." As Jeremias has pointed out, it is also the case that the liturgical and theological expressions associated with Jewish proselyte baptism refer only to adults, even though it is beyond dispute that the children of such proselytes were baptized alongside their parents.[46] Instructions suggesting the prior repentance of the candidate for baptism simply mimic the language of the New Testament, which in no way excludes the contemporaneous baptism of the children (think household baptisms again).

Furthermore, it is probable that early church manuals such as the *Didache* reflect the fact that the church was still living and breathing within its original missionary context. We know that the church was growing quite rapidly throughout the second century, from the relatively small base of believers which it had achieved by the end of the apostolic era. Early church writings were produced within that expanding missionary environment and reflect the language of the Great Commission and Peter's call to "repent and be baptized." Indeed, as will see shortly, McKinion's own presentation of this evidence actually helps to confirm our position.

The only other work from the second century which McKinion cites is the *Apology* of Aristides, which we also introduced above. In arguing for the superiority of Christianity over other religions

---

[45] Ibid., 169-71.
[46] Jeremias, *The Origins of Infant Baptism*, 39-41.

in the empire, Aristides writes of how Christians treat as "brothers and sisters without distinction" those whom they persuade to become Christians from "the servants or the children."[47] McKinion interprets the latter phrase to be referring, not to the children of servants, but to the children of other believers. Thus, he argues that it was only after their conversion that the children of believers were considered a part of the church.[48]

But this is a strained interpretation, to say the least. How would it demonstrate the superiority of Christianity for Christians to treat the *believing* children of other Christians as "brothers and sisters"? Isn't it more natural to read the passage as referring to the children of the servants, who, like their parents, would be considered to be of an inferior class and not entitled to the respect and equal status that would attach to those of the master class, regardless of age? Jeremias' in-depth textual analysis of this portion of Aristides' work yields the same conclusion. He writes, "So then, the conferring of the name 'brother' certainly does not have in view the children of the Christian householders."[49]

Moreover, McKinion does not even mention the passage from Aristides that we quoted above, where he gave testimony to the way in which Christians *gave thanks to God* when a child was born to them, a phrase that he used in the same work to describe the rite of Christian baptism.[50] McKinion also chose not to discuss Irenaeus' remarks from the second century concerning infants that we referenced above.

When we arrive at the close of the second century, McKinion is particularly hard-pressed to deal with the fact that the sources from this time period provide unambiguous testimony to the uniform practice of the church in administering infant baptism. We have already discussed his handling of Tertullian's comments above. We will now take a look at what he has to say about the other sources from the third and fourth centuries.

---

[47] McKinion, 172.
[48] Ibid.
[49] Jeremias, *The Origins of Infant Baptism*, 46.
[50] Jeremias, *Infant Baptism in the First Four Centuries*, 71.

First, he dismisses Hippolytus' comments in *The Apostolic Tradition* about the baptism of infants as confirming only that it was permissible in his "context."[51] Whatever that means, it doesn't seem to do justice to the title of Hippolytus' work.

Second, McKinion does his best to turn the unanimous decision of the synod at Carthage in 253 AD to baptize children on the second or third day of life into an argument *against* infant baptism! Recall that the synod was convened to decide the issue of whether children should be baptized on the eighth day after birth, as with circumcision. McKinion interprets the synod's decision as a possible rejection of the 'baptism as the replacement for circumcision' argument.[52] Given the church's growing concern for administering baptism in a context of very high rates of infant mortality, however, it is not at all clear that their decision should be read that way. But even if that were the case, it is hard to see how the synod's decision could by any stretch of the imagination be considered a rejection of infant baptism.

Third, McKinion treats the comments of Origen in much the same manner as he treated those of Hippolytus. He acknowledges Origen's claim that the practice of infant baptism was a custom handed down from the apostles, but he allows only for the possibility it arose in Palestine in the late second century and thus had found widespread acceptance in the region by the year 250, when Origen wrote.[53] But such comments ignore the fact that Origen had traveled extensively, visiting churches all throughout the empire, and that his claim of apostolic origin would be nonsensical if he had knowledge that the practice was different in other places, or had arisen only in the late second century.

Perhaps the most interesting and illuminating piece of evidence that McKinion offers is one which we did not even mention, because we adjudged it to be from too late a date to be of much use in proving our point that infant baptism was

---

[51] McKinion, 178.
[52] Ibid.
[53] Ibid., 180.

handed down from the apostles. But Dr. McKinion has done us a favor by including it in his essay, albeit it in an attempt to prove the opposite point.

The work in question is called the *Apostolic Constitutions*, which, though composed in the late fourth century, is a compilation of much earlier material. According to McKinion, it is thus "invaluable to our study."[54] In line with his approach to the *Didache* and Justin's *Apology*, Dr. McKinion recites language directed to the catechumen preparing for baptism which called upon him to fast, etc. He then makes this observation: "The one being baptized has already repented, has been cleansed of sin, and has died with Christ."[55]

To this we answer, "Of course he has, because he is a *catechumen*. He is not the infant child of one." This is precisely the point we hinted at a little earlier when we discussed the other two documents that Dr. McKinion relied upon for their adult-directed language. It is important to note that at a fairly early date in the history of the church, it became common in many locales to require a new convert to go through a sometimes lengthy (up to three years!) catechetical period before being admitted to the church (contrary to the biblical example, we might add). Thus, it is not surprising that the church manuals of that era focus a good deal of attention upon the procedures relating to receiving these converts and the preparation which was necessary on their part to be initiated into the church.

The fact that much of the language directed toward those about to receive baptism concerns activities of which only adults (or older children) are capable of performing does not mean that infants are excluded from the rite of baptism. *It simply means that such instructions do not apply to them!*

But if there remains any doubt about the reasonableness of our argument here, let us present one additional quote from the *Apostolic Constitutions* which Dr. McKinion chose to leave out of his discussion. Book VI, Section III contains the following injunction: "also baptize your infants, and bring them up in the

---

[54] Ibid., 182.
[55] Ibid., 181-82.

nurture and admonition of God. For says He, 'Suffer the little children to come unto me, and forbid them not.'"[56]

Thus, the *Apostolic Constitutions* prove that the two separate features (instructions directed to adult catechumens, and the baptism of infants) can, and do, exist side-by-side in the liturgies of the church; there is nothing in the one which suggests exclusion of the other.

The Summary of the Matter

In the matter of what the evidence from church history proves, we must recognize that a certain stand-off exists between the two sides; both Baptists and Reformed Christians tend to view the early evidence as supporting their position. For the Baptist, who argues that infant baptism was an innovation which crept into the church, this means that the apparent lack of explicit instructions for baptizing infants in several writings from the second century demonstrates that the practice had not yet arisen to any great degree. On the other hand, the Reformed Christian, who believes infant baptism to be the biblical model, points to the fact that the earliest unambiguous testimonies to the baptismal practice of the church (Tertullian, Hippolytus, and Origen) are united in affirming the custom of baptizing infants, as well as testifying to its apostolic origin. We might even add the argument that some of the evidence from the second century (Aristides' *Apology* and Irenaeus' comments) is not so ambiguous in its affirmation of infant baptism if one approaches it objectively and without a preconceived point of view.

Nevertheless, when we strip away all of the other arguments and proffers of evidence from either side, we are able to arrive at what amounts to a lowest common denominator in this debate. In fact, it was Dr. McKinion himself who provided it for us. And that basic level of agreement consists in this – by the year 200 AD we have definitive testimony that infant baptism was the normative practice of the church, without any evidence

---

[56] *Ante-Nicene Fathers*, eds. Alexander Roberts and James Donaldson (Peabody, MA: Hendrickson, 2004), 7.457.

whatsoever that a change had taken place during the century immediately preceding that date. Given this agreed-upon starting point, which is the more likely scenario – that believer's baptism was the biblical norm and that it was subsequently changed without any fanfare or debate within 100 years after the last apostle died; or that infant baptism was the tradition handed down by the apostles, and that the unambiguous testimony to that effect from several early church fathers is reliable?

If believer's baptism was the apostolic practice, then we would have to conclude that the scriptural and theoretical basis for it was completely lost to history in less than a century after the apostles left the scene, all without any written testimony to its being overtaken by a different model. Keep in mind that there was not a single voice from the early church who argued that believer's baptism was the apostolic model. Even Tertullian, the first church father to utter a word against infant baptism (and then only as it related to the children of converts from paganism), affirmed its biblical basis.

This is why the evidence we presented from the church fathers is so compelling. Because these events occurred long before the advent of any kind of mass communication, we must account for the fact that the practice of infant baptism was uniform throughout the empire from the earliest point at which we have direct references to it. It would be one thing if we saw only a few churches here and there which adhered to infant baptism, but that is not at all the case. There is no report from anyone that regional or local variations in practice existed. Nor do we have any record of a synod or council having decreed that a change in practice was to be implemented. Rather, the fathers testify not only to its administration in particular locales, but to the geographical uniformity of the practice, as well as its antiquity.

Thus, the most logical conclusion to draw from the evidence is that the testimony of the fathers to the apostolic origin of infant baptism is a reliable record of what really happened in the early church, even though we also begin at an early date to pick up traces of outside influences shaping the church's understanding of what baptism was. The covenantal basis for baptism was gradually eroded until it came to rest almost entirely on the notion of baptismal regeneration.

But, for the most part, the outside (unbiblical) influences tended to move the church more in the direction of a believer's baptism model.[57] The three-year waiting period, the view that post-baptismal sins could not be forgiven, and the borrowing of terms and ideas from the initiation rites of the mystery religions, all contributed to the movement toward postponement of baptism, and served to further confuse the faithful as to its meaning and purpose. Given these pressures, it is remarkable that infant baptism survived at all.[58]

Ironically, it may have been the church's embrace of baptismal regeneration that not only sealed the survival of infant baptism (albeit with a different theological foundation), but also tends to confirm its apostolic origin. After all, it is difficult to conceive of the theology of baptismal regeneration, which begins to appear quite early on, growing out of an original model based upon believer's baptism, with its emphasis upon the prior faith of the recipient. This sort of shift would have required a complete reorientation of the church's theology and practices, and most certainly would have left an indelible impression in the annals of church history. But we find nothing at all in the record to suggest any such change occurred. *In short, our argument from silence keeps piling up!*

In his 1834 work entitled *Infant Baptism Scriptural and Reasonable*, Samuel Miller made this startling observation:

It is an undoubted fact, that the people known in ecclesiastical history under the name of the Anabaptists, who arose in Germany, in the year 1522, were the very first body of people, in the whole Christian world, who rejected the baptism of infants, on the principles now adopted by the Antipaedobaptist body.[59]

---

[57] Peter J. Leithart, "Infant Baptism in History: An Unfinished Tragicomedy," *The Case for Covenantal Infant Baptism*, 257-58.
[58] Ibid., 258.
[59] Samuel Miller, *Infant Baptism Scriptural and Reasonable* (Philadelphia: Presbyterian

There is little doubt that most (if not all) modern Baptists would take issue with this statement. Even a few Reformed Christians have accused Miller of hyperbole for overstating the case.[60] But I am convinced that Miller's carefully chosen words have hit the mark; for even if traces of Baptist thought are detectable in certain writings from the early church, it is still true that there is no evidence of any *body of people* from that time period who held to *the doctrine of believer's baptism as taught by modern Baptists.*

It is instructive that the rite of infant baptism never appeared as the special doctrine of a heretical party or sect in the early church, nor was any sect ever condemned for holding to such a belief.[61] On the contrary, the explicit injunction to baptize infants that we quoted from the *Apostolic Constitutions* appears in the section dealing with heretical forms of baptism which had arisen. Specifically mentioned are the practices of rebaptism and postponement of baptism. Both are condemned as being, not of the "one baptism" into the Lord, but of that "which is conferred by wicked heretics."[62]

In conclusion, perhaps we may restate Dr. Miller's observation in the following language: Reformed Christians may rest comfortably in the knowledge that the evidence from church history confirms our belief that infant baptism was the practice handed down by the apostles, and thus should continue to be our guide as we seek to live faithfully before the Lord, who Himself commanded, "Let the little children come to Me."

Board of Publication, 1834) reprinted in Robert R. Booth, *Children of the Promise: The Biblical Case for Infant Baptism* (Phillipsburg, NJ: P&R, 1995), 168.

[60] See, e.g., Leithart, 249-50. Leithart quotes Gregory of Nazianzus as saying that it was permissible to baptize children provided that they could "take in something of the mystery, and answer …, and even if they do not yet understand fully, can nevertheless retain some impression." To Leithart, "That sounds a lot like a modern Baptist argument." But does it really? How many modern Baptists would be satisfied to administer the rite of baptism to one who did not yet understand fully, but was capable only of retaining "some impression" of their baptism? Moreover, Leithart fails to mention that Gregory placed that magic age at only three years old, and further advocated the baptism of all infants who were in mortal danger (Jeremias, *Infant Baptism*, 96). Perhaps it is Leithart who is guilty of hyperbole.

[61] Jeremias, *Infant Baptism in the First Four Centuries*, 57.

[62] *Ante-Nicene Fathers*, 7.456.

Chapter 7

Infant Baptism as a Sign and Seal

Having spent our time thus far looking at the case for infant baptism, we now seek to answer the more fundamental questions concerning just what baptism is, and what it is meant to accomplish. While the subject matter may be in the realm of elementary principles, it is precisely at this point that far too many Reformed Christians stumble, for in their failure to understand what Baptism is, and what it signifies, they find themselves hard-pressed to make the case for baptizing the infant children of the covenant.

The relative lack of uniformity in the way in which Reformed writers have addressed the subject over the years is no doubt at least partly to blame for the confusion that exists amongst Christians trying to rightly understand the nature of baptism. What one writer refers to as the meaning of baptism another will call its symbolism, and vice versa, while another will refer to the purpose of baptism in terms that a different writer has labeled its essence. Even the most basic of terms used to define baptism, *sign* and *seal*, are themselves often defined quite differently from one source to the next.

As an extreme example of this tendency, we find in a single chapter from an otherwise helpful book on infant baptism the author making reference to, or attempting to distinguish between, each of these related concepts: 1) the meaning of baptism; 2) the significance of baptism; 3) the central content of baptism; 4) the principal element of baptism; 5) the true foundation of baptism; 6) the basis for baptism; 7) the thing represented in baptism; 8) the cause of baptism; 9) the reason and motive for the giving of the sign; and finally, 10) the fulfillment of baptism.

Nevertheless, it is important to note that there is no substantive disagreement amongst Reformed theologians over the essential meaning and purpose of baptism, since almost all of the same ideas are present in any extended discussion of the subject, even though there is wide variation in assigning the different ideas present to one of these categories. Of course, the problem is that these ideas are, for the most part, intertwined, and it is not easy (nor perhaps always helpful) to attempt to differentiate between them.

Though we too will venture into these waters, we will attempt to provide a simple, concise definition and understanding of baptism which represents a composite or consensus reading of the multitude of ideas out there. In order to do so we will lean heavily upon the Westminster Confession of Faith (WCF) and the Westminster Larger Catechism (WLC). Both of these documents were prepared by the Scottish and English Reformers who met in London between 1643 and 1648 for the purpose of composing a summary of the content and teaching of Scripture that all Christians could study and embrace.

By saying that we aim to set forth a simple and concise definition of baptism and its purposes, we do not mean to imply that the subject matter is not worthy of extended discussion, or that baptism is not so rich in its meaning and significance as to be incapable of producing divergent opinions and emphases concerning its administration. But we strive for brevity and simplicity here, and so our goal will be to provide a definition and description of baptism and its purposes that will be short and to the point, while covering all the bases in the process.

The Meaning and Purpose of Baptism

WLC 165 defines baptism as follows:

> Baptism is a sacrament of the New Testament, wherein Christ hath ordained the washing with water in the name of the Father, and of the Son, and of the Holy Ghost, to be a sign and seal of ingrafting into himself, of remission of sins by his blood, and regeneration by his Spirit; of adoption and resurrection unto everlasting life; and whereby the parties baptized are solemnly admitted into the visible church, and enter into an open and professed engagement to be wholly and only the Lord's.

This statement from the Catechism provides most of the information we need to answer the three questions that concern us here: 1) What is baptism?; 2) What is its essential meaning?; and 3) What is its purpose?

What is baptism?

In the first place, baptism is a "sacrament of the New Testament." The WCF (27:1) defines the sacraments as "holy signs and seals of the covenant of grace." Thus, at its most basic level, baptism is a sign and seal of the covenant of grace, which takes place when the recipient is "washed with water" in the Name of the Triune God.

What is the essential meaning of baptism?

The essential meaning conveyed in baptism is union with Christ. The Catechism refers to the believer's "ingrafting" into Christ, as well as the more particular benefits that accompany this union: remission of sins by his blood, regeneration by his Spirit, adoption, and resurrection unto everlasting life.[1] All of these benefits flow from the union with Christ that is the essence of baptism.

---

[1] Johannes G. Vos, *The Westminster Larger Catechism: A Commentary*, ed. G.I. Williamson (Phillipsburg, NJ: P&R, 2002), 472.

The act of washing with water is intended to symbolize cleansing or purification, as wrought by the Holy Spirit, who is pictured as being poured out upon the recipient of baptism (Tit. 3:5-6; Eph. 5:26). Because Christ is holy, all those who would be united to Him must be cleansed from their sin. Baptism is a picture of that cleansing.

What is the purpose of baptism? What does it accomplish for the recipient?

Baptism accomplishes three things on behalf of the recipient. First, it provides for the solemn admission of the recipient into the visible church. Baptism marks off the recipient as one who has been separated from the world at large and placed under the care and authority of Christ and His church. Yet the Westminster Standards are clear that baptism is merely the formal and public (i.e., solemn) recognition of those who are already church members in God's sight "by reason of their covenant standing (in the case of infants) or by reason of their own profession of faith in Christ and obedience to him (in the case of adults)."[2] At the same time, the recipient of baptism enters into "an open and professed engagement to be wholly and only the Lord's."

Second, baptism serves as a "sign and seal" to the recipient of the benefits of Christ's mediation on his behalf. This assertion is based upon the text of Romans 4:11, where Paul says that Abraham "received the sign of circumcision, a seal of the righteousness of the faith which he had while still uncircumcised, that he might be the father of all who believe, though they are uncircumcised, that righteousness might be imputed to them also." Since baptism has replaced circumcision as the sign of the covenant in this dispensation, what Paul says here about circumcision is just as true about baptism – it is a sign and seal of the righteousness of faith.

But what does it mean to say that baptism is a sign and seal? And what does it mean to say that it is a sign and seal of the *righteousness of faith*? As a sign, baptism is a visible testimony to

---

[2] Ibid., 474.

God's grace, calling upon the recipient (as well as all those who are witnesses thereto) to remember God's promise in the gospel and to be assured of its fulfillment. As a seal, baptism serves to authenticate and confirm this promise of righteousness through faith that God has given to His people in the gospel.

Although seals are not as familiar to us today, they were very important to those who lived in centuries past. The authenticity of a royal document or decree was attested by whether or not it contained the king's seal, which was added when he pressed his signet ring into the hot wax, thus making an imprint which was identifiable to all. Jesus used this imagery when he told the people in Galilee that they should trust in Him because God the Father had "set His seal on Him" (John 6:27). Baptism serves as Christ's seal on the authenticity of the gospel promises.

But if it be argued that God's promises do not need authentication in our eyes, that they are sufficiently real and secure in themselves apart from any additional testimony or confirmation, we answer that this is God's way of condescending to our weakness.[3] The sign of baptism is not something that God needs to add to His promises in order to make them real, or to remind Him of whom are those within the sphere of the covenant. Rather, baptism is given to us *for our benefit*. It is a visible reminder and testimony to us of God's faithfulness, and of His promise to acquit all those who have faith in Christ. It is, as Romans 4:11 says, "a seal of the righteousness of the faith" which Abraham had.

But now it behooves us to take a closer look at the meaning of those words, for it is at this very point that many Christians get tripped up. They tend to assume that what is being sealed in baptism is the faith of the person being baptized, even as the reason for Abraham's circumcision was to validate and seal his faith, as if God was attesting to its genuineness and placing His stamp of approval on it.[4] But this cannot be the case, for if we understand circumcision and baptism in this manner, then

---

[3] Murray, 84.

[4] Mark E. Ross, "Baptism and Circumcision as Signs and Seals," *The Case for Covenantal Infant Baptism*, 90.

we are unable to explain why the covenant sign was applied to Ishmael, Abraham's firstborn son, when God had already disclosed that he was not going to be a recipient of the covenant promises (Gen. 17:19-27). For that matter, we would not be able to explain why the sign was given to any of the infant seed of Abraham or his descendants without reference to their faith as already being in existence. As Mark Ross points out, "If circumcision is taken directly as a sign and seal of faith, or of imputed righteousness, or of an inward spiritual transformation, it fails miserably."[5]

Nor does this problem go away by adopting the believer's baptism model espoused by our Baptist friends, as proven by the example of Simon the Sorcerer (Acts 8) and countless others after him who received the sign of baptism as adults and later proved to be unconverted.[6] But the dilemma proves to be a manufactured one when we come to understand Paul's words aright. For we have misunderstood him if we take his words to mean that God's giving of the sign of circumcision was in *response* to Abraham's faith.

The critical point of distinction is this: it is not Abraham's faith which is sealed in his circumcision, but the *righteousness* of that faith. That is what Paul says in Romans 4:11. God seals his promise to Abraham (and us through him) that all of those who have faith in Christ *will be counted as righteous on the day of judgment*. It is the adequacy and sufficiency of Abraham's faith to which God attests in the rite of circumcision. Because circumcision testifies to God's covenant faithfulness, what is certified in the dispensing of the rite is not so much a truth about Abraham, or any other person receiving it, but a truth about God.[7]

Thus, the meaning and purpose of the sign of the covenant is precisely the same in the case of infants as it is in the case of adults. For God has given His people signs to serve as visible reminders of *His faithfulness*, not ours. B.B. Warfield responded

---

[5] Ibid., 91.
[6] Ibid., 92.
[7] Ibid., 94.

to the man-centered view of baptism which is prevalent in our culture today in this way:

> Baptism, as circumcision, is a gift of God to his people, not of his people to God. Abraham did not bring circumcision to God; he "received" it from God. God gave it to him as a "sign" and a "seal," not to others but to himself. It is inadequate, therefore, to speak of baptism as "the badge of a Christian man's profession" ... The witness of baptism is not to others but to ourselves; and it is not by us but by God that the witness is borne.[8]

Finally, as a sacrament, baptism is designed to strengthen and increase our faith (WLC 162). The fact that some who are recipients of the sign may not as yet possess such faith does not detract from this understanding one bit, since the strengthening of our faith through the right use of the sacraments is a lifelong process. This means that every time we are witness to a baptism or participate in the taking of the Lord's Supper, our faith is nourished by the Word of God which accompanies it and testifies to His goodness.

Moreover, God's covenant signs testify not only to the blessings of the covenant of grace, but to its corresponding curses as well. This is why the understanding of baptism we laid out above is the only one which does not call God's promises into question by the later unbelief of one who has undergone the rite. God's word will stand: those who believe will be accounted righteous, and those who do not will be cut-off.[9] And because the children of believing parents are included along with them in the sphere of the covenant, this promise of blessing (and threatened curse) is just as much for them as for their parents.

---

[8] Benjamin B. Warfield, *Selected Shorter Writings*, ed. John E. Meeter (Phillipsburg, NJ: P&R, 2001), 1:327.

[9] Ross, 95.

The Efficacy of Baptism

It should be clear from the previous comments that the rite of baptism does not save anyone. It does not affect the union with Christ which is pictured in the act. Nor was it designed to do so. Rather, union with Christ and salvation from sin is based upon the sovereign, electing choice of God, who "has mercy on whom He wills" (Rom. 9:18).

Nor is reception of the rite of baptism necessary for salvation, as some who have misread Mark 16:16 have asserted. WCF 28:5 says of baptism: "Although it be a great sin to contemn or neglect this ordinance, yet grace and salvation are not so inseparably annexed unto it, as that no person can be regenerated, or saved, without it; or, that all that are baptized are undoubtedly regenerated." Thus, baptism is neither necessary for salvation, nor does it insure that the one who has received it is actually saved.

But this does not mean that baptism is a bare sign or empty seal.[10] On the contrary, we assert that baptism is efficacious in conferring the grace which it signifies to those whom God has actually chosen. This is the way in which the matter is stated in WCF 28:6:

> The efficacy of Baptism is not tied to that moment of time wherein it is administered; yet, notwithstanding, by the right use of this ordinance, the grace promised is not only offered, but really exhibited, and conferred, by the Holy Ghost, to such (whether of age or infants) as that grace belongeth unto, according to the counsel of God's own will, in his appointed time.

Because we do not limit the efficacy of baptism to the moment of its administration only, we may affirm that it will never fail to confer the grace which it exhibits, even though possession of the thing signified may not take place until many years after

---

[10] Alan D. Strange, "Baptism in Our Confessional Standards," *New Horizons in the Orthodox Presbyterian Church* (March 2008), 4.

the administration of the sign. It will happen, as the Confession states, in God's "appointed time."

The Confession's careful wording, however, makes it clear that this grace is conferred only upon those to whom it belongs – the elect whom God has chosen in eternity past. As we stated back in chapter three, it is only they who actually receive the benefits pictured in baptism, for it is only with them that the covenant is truly made.[11]

Does this mean, then, that we should seek to be as certain as possible of someone's election before dispensing the rite of baptism to them? Should we, in effect, adopt the believer's baptism model, but with even more stringent criteria for gauging the genuineness and lasting character of the candidate's faith? What about returning to the practice of some early churches in requiring a three-year waiting period before one can become a member? Of course, we have already answered such questions sufficiently to demonstrate their absurdity. The biblical examples of Abraham's circumcision of Ishmael, and Isaac's of Esau, should be enough to silence such arguments.

It is important to note that no one, not even a mature adult, is ever baptized because they are presumed saved. They are baptized because they fall into one of the classes of people that God has commanded *shall* receive the sign of the covenant. Those who do so are adults who have not previously received the sign, and are presently confessing Christ as Lord, *and their children.*

As one who participates in the examination of prospective church members, it is possible that I might at some point harbor a private presumption about the genuineness (or lack thereof) of a particular individual's testimony of faith, but such private thoughts cannot be the basis for withholding the covenant sign from one who otherwise gives a credible profession of faith in Christ, and whose life's walk does not call such profession into doubt. Regardless of what may happen later, or what the true

---

[11] It is for this reason that some theologians distinguish between the internal and external aspects of the covenant of grace, noting that all who are in the visible church enjoy (at least to some extent) the external aspects of the covenant, but that only the elect are in the covenant internally as well. Ibid., 3-4.

state of that person's soul may be, the duty to baptize is clear. Thankfully, God has relieved the officers of His church from the responsibility of having omniscience in these matters.

We baptize our children not because we presume them to be saved (though we may have good reason for doing just that), but because God has commanded us to do so, and because He has promised to be a God to us and to our descendants after us. The fact that some of them may at a future point in time reject the blessings offered in this covenant does not change this formula one bit, nor does it make God out to be a liar. God does truly make His covenant with, and bring to faith, those of our children who are elect, whether the regenerative act takes place at the time of baptism or at some point in time much later. Thus, the baptism of our children is an act of faith on our part; it reflects a desire to be obedient to God's command, and a trusting in His promise to be God to us *and to our descendants*.[12]

The Mode of Baptism

The subject of the mode of baptism has generated a great deal of heat over the centuries. Whole books have been written on the subject, and more than a few works on baptism allot a significant percentage of their total space to a discussion of the issue.[13] But because our interest here is framed along the more narrow lines of the validity of, and biblical warrant for, infant baptism in particular, our treatment of this subject need not be a lengthy one.

---

[12] As a practical matter, it should be emphasized that, although we do not baptize our covenant children because we presume them to be saved, we are nevertheless to view and treat them as such, rearing them in the nurture and admonition of the Lord. The view which is all too common today, that the children of believers are merely put in a more favorable position to be saved by their own act of conversion at some later point in time, is *not* the historic Reformed position. Such a view ignores the fact that the promise of the covenant has been made not only to parents, but also to their seed. Thus, "the proper approach to, and rearing of, them by parents and church is 'Christian nurture,' not the demand of the dramatic conversion experience characteristic of revivals." Engelsma, 35-36, with further citation to Lewis Bevens Schenck, *The Presbyterian Doctrine of Children in the Covenant: An Historical Study of the Significance of Infant Baptism in the Presbyterian Church* (Phillipsburg, N.J.: P&R, 2003), 127, 145.

[13] As an example, John Murray's book *Christian Baptism* devotes more than one-fourth of its pages to this topic.

Those unfamiliar with the debate may wonder what all the fuss is about. After all, is it really that critical how the waters of baptism are actually applied to the recipient? Isn't it adequate to determine who should receive the rite and not worry so much about the form in which it is administered? Frankly, I must admit of a certain inclination to agree with such sentiments. On the other hand, as we shall see, the debate does touch upon our understanding of the very essence of baptism – its meaning and purpose. And in that respect it also touches upon the question of who are the proper subjects of baptism.

By and large the debate over the mode of baptism centers on whether or not *immersion* is the only acceptable form of baptism (as most Baptists would argue), or whether there are other equally valid forms which may be used. Baptismal immersion consists in the placing of the individual completely under the water and lifting them out again. Obviously, the administration of immersion is more cumbersome than the traditional method which involves placing water from a baptismal font on the head of the person being baptized. Immersion requires the presence of a baptistery or standing body of water to be effectively administered.

On what basis do Baptists maintain that immersion is the only valid mode of baptism? Typically, they argue on the basis of two points: 1) that the Greek term for baptism (*baptizo*) always refers to immersion; and 2) that the primary symbolic character of baptism is the recipient's imitation of Christ's death, burial, and resurrection.[14] It remains for us now to see whether or not either of these arguments can withstand biblical scrutiny.

First, it is simply not true that the word *baptizo* means to immerse. This is easily proven by reference to a few of the places in the New Testament where the word appears and the context makes it obvious that immersion cannot be the intended meaning. In Hebrews 9:10, for example, we are told that the Old Testament ceremonial law contained "various washings" (baptisms), and then

---

[14] Joseph Pipa, "The Mode of Baptism," *The Case for Covenantal Infant Baptism*, 112-13; cf. Murray, 6.

we are reminded that these baptisms included the sprinkling of the blood of bulls and goats (9:13), the sprinkling of the book and all the people (9:19), and the sprinkling of the tabernacle and the vessels of the ministry (9:21).[15] Clearly, then, the word baptism cannot be equated with immersion.

Another example occurs in the opening chapters of Acts, where Jesus promised the disciples that they would be "baptized with the Holy Spirit" in a few days (1:5). When the promised baptism arrived, Peter described it (quoting the prophet Joel) as a pouring out (2:18). Obviously, no water at all was involved in this baptism. But more importantly, this baptism signifies "union" with the Holy Spirit, the concept which we have already demonstrated is at the very heart of what baptism means.

The concept of union is also present in 1 Cor. 10:1-2,[16] a passage which runs so thoroughly contrary to the Baptist argument that it should be an embarrassment to them. Paul used the imagery of baptism to describe the union which Moses and the people of Israel achieved by virtue of their "passing through the sea" together. What is so fascinating (and pertinent) about this particular passage is that it was the Israelites who were said to have been baptized in the sea, even though it was the Egyptians who were immersed!

Even some of the Baptists' favorite passages, the ones which they have always been quick to point out, do not prove that the baptisms spoken of there involved immersion. A prime example is that of the Ethiopian eunuch, whose story is told at Acts 8:26-40. Baptists love to point out that the text says that Philip and the eunuch "went down into the water" and then "came up out of the water." What they seem to miss altogether, however, is that Luke tells us that *both of the men* went down into, and came up out of, the water. What is said about the eunuch in this respect is also said about Philip. Surely our Baptist friends do not believe that Philip baptized himself as well as the eunuch! But if we understand their argument correctly, it is Luke's conscious choice of prepositions

[15] G.I. Williamson, *The Westminster Confession of Faith for Study Classes* (Philadelphia: P&R, 1964), 210.
[16] Pipa, 119.

here that proves the eunuch's immersion. And if that is so, why would Luke choose to describe the action as a combined one? John Murray commented on this passage as follows:

> It is not now maintained that Philip did not immerse the eunuch when he baptised him. That may have been the mode in this case. But what is to be recognised is – a fact too frequently ignored in the Baptist argumentation – that this passage does not prove immersion. The expressions "they both went down into the water" and "they came up out of the water" are satisfied by the thought that they both went down to the water, stood on the brink or stepped into the edge, and that Philip baptised the eunuch by scooping up the water and pouring it or sprinkling it on him. This is *all* that can be shown to have occurred. As far as the going into, and coming up out of, the water are concerned nothing is stated in respect of the eunuch that is not also in respect of Philip himself. Hence there is no proof of immersion in this passage. What the actual mode was we simply do not know, and this text does not support the Baptist contention.[17]

Indeed, even if Luke's words were meant to convey that the eunuch (along with Philip) went *into* the water, and not merely *down to* the water, it would still not prove that he was immersed *under* the water.[18] Pictorial representations of baptisms from the early centuries often show those being baptized as standing in water and having the waters of baptism poured on them.[19]

[17] Murray, 24.

[18] Actually, the whole Baptist argument at this point is built on a false foundation. William Shishko writes, "[T]he Greek prepositions translated 'into' and 'out of' may also mean 'to,' 'toward,' or 'unto,' and 'from' or 'away from.' In fact, in Acts 8, the Greek preposition *eis* is used eleven times, but only once (vs. 38) is it commonly translated 'into.' In verses 3, 5, 16, 25, 26, 27, and 40, it is best translated as 'to.' Similarly, we should understand that when Philip baptized the Ethiopian eunuch, he went 'to' the water, dipped his hand into it, and sprinkled the eunuch, identifying him with the Messiah and his cleansing work ..." William Shishko, "Is Immersion Necessary for Baptism?," *New Horizons in the Orthodox Presbyterian Church* (July-August 2000). Accessed September 24, 2008. Online: http://www.opc.org/nh.html?article_id=278.

[19] Louis Berkhof, *Systematic Theology* (Grand Rapids: Eerdmans, 1996), 631.

The point we are making here is not that immersion is not a valid mode of baptism, but that the expression "to baptize" does not mean "to immerse." There are many more examples that could be adduced to help demonstrate the point, but it would be superfluous to do so. Frankly, the evidence against the Baptist contention here is so overwhelming (and devastatingly plain) that I am amazed they persist in their efforts to advance it.

The second argument they put forth in their case for immersion is more substantive, but also one which we have addressed to some extent already. It is argued that Baptism is primarily intended to symbolize regeneration by the recipient's "dying and rising again," which is pictured in the act of going under the water and coming up again. Two passages of Scripture, Col. 2:11-12 and Rom. 6:3-6, are usually appealed to in support of this contention. But neither of those passages is concerned with prescribing (or even describing) a mode of baptism. Rather, when Paul writes that we have been "buried with Him in baptism" (Col. 2:12), or that those of us who were "baptized into Christ Jesus were baptized into His death" (Rom. 6:3), he is not describing a mode for baptism, but emphasizing the fact that when we undergo baptism we are united to Him. That is what he means by saying that we are baptized "into" Christ. In these passages, Paul most assuredly refers to the spiritual effects of baptism.

When we are united to Christ we become partakers of all the benefits which flow from His death and resurrection on our behalf. In that way we are "buried with Him" and "baptized into His death." Baptism signifies that this union has taken place (Gal. 3:27), through the purification from sin which the waters of baptism symbolize. If the mode of baptism was intended to symbolize a burial and resurrection, as Baptists argue, then why is water used at all? Isn't it more likely that God has given us a covenant sign which resembles that which it was intended to signify?

Baptism is not primarily a picture of dying and being raised, but one of being cleansed from sin (John 3:22-26; Acts 22:16; 1 Cor. 6:11; Tit. 3:5; Rev. 1:5). And the fact that this cleansing is often portrayed in Scripture as a pouring or sprinkling is evident from many passages as well (Num. 8:7; Isa. 44:3; Ezek. 36:25; Heb. 9:10; 1 Pet. 1:2). Because baptism signifies our initiation into the benefits of Christ's mediation on our behalf, we are made partakers of His death, burial, and resurrection, but we do not *imitate* His dying and being raised when we submit to it.

Reformed Christians have generally held that, as long as the fundamental idea of purification finds expression in the rite, the mode of baptism is immaterial.[20] Thus, the Westminster Confession of Faith (28:3) states that, "Dipping of the person into the water is not necessary; but Baptism is rightly administered by pouring, or sprinkling water upon the person." Although the Confession's statement does not condemn the practice of immersion, the preference for pouring or sprinkling is obvious. This is perfectly appropriate, given the fact that these two modes are the predominant ones found in Scripture to describe the work of cleansing from sin and regeneration by the Holy Spirit. Thus, pouring and sprinkling are surely the more proper modes of baptism.

In this regard, then, Reformed Christians have been much more ecumenical in practice than the vast majority of Baptists, who will not recognize the validity of a prior baptism (even of an adult) that was not administered by immersion. Given that Jesus did not prescribe a particular mode of baptism, such a policy is (at best) unwise, and (at worst) a bare form of legalism.

Rebaptism

Because Baptists do not recognize infant baptisms, or even the prior baptism of any adult who was not immersed, they insist on rebaptism before the person may be admitted to membership and allowed to partake of the Lord's Supper.

In contrast to that position, WCF 28:7 says, "The sacrament of Baptism is but once to be administered unto any person." Though the words of the Confession are plain enough on their face, they leave open the question of what constitutes valid Christian baptism in the first instance. That is, what are the

---

[20] Berkhof, 629.

criteria for determining whether or not someone has already received baptism? Because the Confession did not address that issue directly, there has been a lack of uniformity in applying the provisions of this section over the centuries. John Calvin had argued in his *Institutes of the Christian Religion* that so long as the baptism had been performed in the name of the Father, Son, and Holy Spirit, it should be considered to have been Christian baptism. Thus, rebaptism in such cases was unnecessary, regardless of the orthodoxy (or lack thereof) of either the minister or the tradition from which he came.

It might be reasonable to assume that this was the understanding which the Westminster divines had in mind in composing this section of the Confession. After all, the influence of Calvin's writings on both the Reformation movement in general, and the Westminster Assembly in particular, is undeniable. But not all have interpreted the Confession's statement in line with Calvin's urging. For example, in 1845 the General Assembly of the Presbyterian Church (Old School) in the United States voted almost unanimously to declare that Roman Catholic baptism was not valid Christian baptism. James Henley Thornwell, a Presbyterian minister of that time, noted that to hold as Calvin urged was akin to treating the name of the Trinity as a magic incantation, when the essence of baptism consisted in professing the *faith* of the Trinity.[21]

But whatever may have been the intention of the Westminster divines on this particular point, it is clear, when this section is combined with that on the mode of baptism, that they meant to answer the Anabaptist call for rebaptism in no uncertain terms. Indeed, it is not unreasonable to assume that Calvin's views on rebaptism were influenced by his utter disdain for the Anabaptist view that all previous baptisms not administered by immersion, and to adult believers only, were invalid.[22] It has been said (with a

---

[21] John W. Robbins, "Sacramental Sorcery," *The Trinity Review* (October 2006), 3-4.

[22] Calvin's desire to oppose the doctrine of the Anabaptists was probably also to blame for his denial that John's disciples were rebaptized, and his argument that John's baptism was equivalent to Christian baptism, a position which nearly all Reformed expositors since him have denied.

great deal of seriousness) that both Luther and Calvin had more choice words of contempt for the Anabaptists of their day, than for the Church of Rome. The Westminster Confession of Faith probably reflects that same priority by more directly addressing the Anabaptist theology in its chapter on baptism.

In his book *What Do Presbyterians Believe?*, Gordon Clark relates a story so absurd it seems almost comedic:

> A devout friend of mine attended one of those Bible Schools in which a knowledge of the Bible was neither too profound nor too extensive. There he was persuaded to be immersed; and he became a Baptist minister. A small church wanted his part time services; but they insisted that he permit them to immerse him, for there was no telling whether the Bible school had done a good job or not. So my friend, easy going and desirous of ministering to a neglected congregation, was immersed a second time. Some years later the preaching arrangement terminated, and a Baptist congregation was formed in a village much nearer my friend's home. He had other religious work and was not available to act as pastor; but the people and the pastor they called wanted him to join as a member. He was glad to do so, for this would help another Baptist congregation to get started. But before they would receive him as a communicant member, they insisted that they should immerse him, since there was no telling how good his previous immersions were. At this point my friend decided that two immersions were really enough. He would help the congregation; he would attend; but he would not join.[23]

Hopefully, it is unnecessary to point out that we see nothing like this on the pages of Scripture. The attitude toward baptism reflected in this story is not just unbiblical; it betrays a view of the sacrament that is pure ritualistic formalism. There is no concern whatsoever about the action of God in baptism; rather, the focus is entirely upon the correctness of its administration. Immersion

[23] Gordon H. Clark, *What Do Presbyterians Believe?* (Philipsburg, NJ: P&R, 1965), 243-44.

is the *only thing* that matters! But this attitude is completely at odds with the biblical meaning and model.

I now regret undergoing my own rebaptism in 1995. Though it was done in ignorance of the principles which we have laid out here, I cannot help but wish that I had not cast aside my first baptism as if it had been inadequate to account for my newfound faith. I wish I had understood back then that my lack of devotion to the Lord between the time of my first baptism, and my coming to faith all those years later, did not invalidate the promises sealed to me then. I wish that I had not demanded of God that He reaffirm and re-seal those promises a second time, nor used my prior ignorance and failure to appreciate those promises as an excuse to treat baptism as the "badge of a Christian man's profession."

Calvin was correct to pose the question, "if ignorance vitiates a previous baptism so that it must be corrected by a second baptism … what rivers would suffice to repeat as many immersions as the instances of ignorance that are daily corrected in us through the Lord's mercy?"[24] As Calvin points out, I will never be *worthy* of receiving baptism, for I am in need of constant cleansing from the sin that still clings to me. Thankfully, the blood of Christ, shed on my behalf, provides the cleansing that I need – *just as God had promised me in my first baptism*. All the intervening years of ignorance and neglect of His means of grace did not vitiate that promise. God brought to pass the reality pictured there *in His own appointed time*.

Improving our Baptism

Instead of repeating our baptism, we should seek to put it to good use each and every day of our lives by giving serious and thankful consideration to its nature, and the ends to which it was instituted. This is what the delegates to the Westminster Assembly referred to as *improving* our baptism. The phrase may seem like a strange one, for certainly there is no improving upon

---

[24] John Calvin, *Institutes of the Christian Religion*, ed. John T. McNeill, trans. Ford Lewis Battles (Philadelphia: Westminster, 1960), 4.15.18.

the rite itself, or upon the benefits which it is meant to confer. But improving our baptism refers to the idea of drawing upon those benefits in a conscious way, for the purpose of growing in holiness and assurance of faith.

WLC 167 states the matter this way:

> The needful but much neglected duty of improving our Baptism, is to be performed by us all our life long, especially in the time of temptation, and when we are present at the administration of it to others; by serious and thankful consideration of the nature of it, and of the ends for which Christ instituted it, the privileges and benefits conferred and sealed thereby, and our solemn vow made therein; ...

As the Confession states, improving our baptism is a "much neglected duty." If that was true in the church of the 1600s, it is even more so in our own day. Baptism is too often seen as nothing more than an external religious rite with little significance beyond the moment of its administration. The thought that it would actually serve to influence our daily engagements and give strength to our faith is probably considered by many to be a quaint expression of religious optimism.

No doubt at least some of those who have opposed the baptism of infants have done so on the erroneous ground that, since infants are incapable of receiving any of its promised benefits at the moment of administration, the rite thus serves no useful purpose in their case.[25] But this sort of thinking, which we have already answered adequately, represents a horrible misunderstanding of the meaning and purposes of baptism in the first place. It also has the effect of considerably cheapening the significance of baptism in the case of adults.

This notion of improving our baptism is an important one, for God did not provide His people with a covenant sign that was intended to be of significance to them for only one brief

---

[25] Vos, 480.

moment of their lives and then forgotten about. Rather, we should be reminded of our baptism, and the "privileges and benefits conferred and sealed thereby," each and every day of our lives, as we struggle with the sins and temptations that continue to plague us. Martin Luther, when facing his own temptations, would often reply, "I am a baptized man," which was his vivid way of reminding himself that he possessed all that he needed to resist the devil and joyfully serve his Lord.[26]

So too are we to draw daily strength from our own baptism. In the same way that circumcision was a visible reminder to every Israelite male throughout his entire life, so now should our baptism serve as a continual reminder of God's grace and favor toward us. Although our own baptism may not be visible to us in the same sense, it is in a different sense 'before our very eyes' every time we have the privilege of witnessing another covenant child receive the blessings of their own baptism.

Christ's death on the cross put an end once and for all to the shedding of blood in relation to the work of redemption. As a result, circumcision is no longer an appropriate sign and seal for the children of God. But we now have an even better sign in this age of greater grace; one which is administered to male and female alike, to be a constant (and yes, visible) reminder of our inheritance.

Baptism is a sign and seal of the covenant of grace. And because this covenant includes the children of believers, the sign is just as much for them as for their parents. They are thereby marked out as belonging to the Lord, and from that day forth set out on the lifelong journey to *improve* on that baptism which they have received. By the grace of God that is signed and sealed at their baptism, they are empowered to do just that.

---

[26] Strange, 5.

Chapter 8

The Reformation and Infant Baptism

An old familiar proverb states that the darkest hour of the night occurs just prior to the light of dawn. And so it was with the state of the institutional church at the beginning of the sixteenth century, in the years just before the Reformation broke over Europe. Though the Christian religion had become firmly entrenched on European soil, and had a sizeable presence in certain lands to the east as well, the visible church was mired in scandal and loaded down with various unbiblical practices and ideas. Many of the popes, cardinals, bishops, and priests of that time period had fallen into gross and open immorality, bringing shame and disgrace upon the church and causing many of the faithful to question its authority in spiritual matters for the first time.

Theologically, the Roman church had been undergoing change for centuries, moving further and further away from the biblical teachings on grace and salvation. The development was gradual, but by the beginning of the sixteenth century, it had built a theological and sacramental system which had the effect of undermining personal assurance of salvation and kept individual Christians ever in pursuit of the intercessory benefits that the church dispensed at its discretion (sometimes only when the right sums of money had been paid). Thus, the faithful found themselves on an endless performance treadmill, always in doubt as to whether or not they had done enough to merit salvation from their sins.

This departure from the teachings of the Bible had reached into the realm of the sacraments as well. While the medieval church had retained the apostolic practice of baptizing infants, the rite had taken on an entirely different character than had prevailed in the early church. Baptism had become completely detached from its covenantal moorings and was presented by the church as possessing almost magical status, being the instrument whereby regeneration and initial justification was actually accomplished in all who received it (i.e., baptismal regeneration). In reality, however, the rite had degenerated into one of bare ceremony, since it was neither accompanied by the pure Word of God, nor was the biblical faith of the parents who presented their children for baptism a necessary prerequisite any longer.

It was into this spiritual darkness that God sent the great Reformers of the sixteenth century, the most famous of whom were Martin Luther, Ulrich Zwingli, John Calvin and John Knox. These men, along with their spiritual allies and successors, set about reforming the medieval church's theology and practices, and through their efforts, by the middle of the century there was a thriving Reformed community of believers in almost every nation in Europe. Indeed, in a few places the Reformed faith had already become dominant.

In addition to restoring the biblical gospel to its rightful place in the preaching and teaching ministry of the church, the Reformers eliminated or replaced numerous aspects of worship, some of which were simply contrary to the commands of Scripture, while others were downright idolatrous. The rite of baptism received its own reinterpretation at the hands of the Reformers, who (with the exception of Luther) unanimously rejected baptismal regeneration and recaptured its essence as a sign and seal of the covenant of grace. Furthermore, they (Luther included) argued that, as a visible symbol and means of grace, baptism was not truly biblical baptism unless it was accompanied by the proclamation of the gospel. After all, it was the promise contained in the gospel that baptism was intended to visibly represent and seal.

While Luther's views on the significance of baptism may have differed somewhat from the rest of the Reformers who followed on his heels, to a man they were united in their insistence that infant baptism was biblical, and that the children of believing parents were entitled to receive the sign by virtue of their having been born into the covenant. It was this rediscovery of the covenantal understanding of infant baptism that formed the ground upon which all of the great Reformed confessions of the sixteenth and seventeenth centuries based their theologies of baptism (and infant baptism in particular).

Of course, there were some dissenters who arose to challenge the theology of Reformed baptism during this time period. The forerunners of today's Baptists, they were known primarily by the name Anabaptists ("re-baptizers"), although Luther and some of the other Reformers referred to them with even more derogatory names. Although they professed a number of distinctive tenets that set them apart from the general strain of Reformed theology in the sixteenth century, it was their opposition to infant baptism, in favor of believer's baptism, that gave them their name and also engendered severe criticism, and even persecution, of their leaders in a few places.[1]

In common with today's Baptists, they argued that baptism was to be administered only to those who had already placed their trust in Christ and made specific request for it. They argued that this was in keeping with the "testimony of the apostles," and that infant baptism was actually "the highest and chief abomination

---

[1] The Anabaptists were not a completely homogeneous community. But most of them, in addition to opposing infant baptism, also opposed any involvement in civil affairs, were pacifistic, and argued for the complete separation of church and state. A few were even avowedly revolutionary and advocated an early form of communism. In many of these ways, then, they differed considerably from most Baptists of today.

of the pope."[2] Aside from these few terse statements found in the Schleitheim Confession of 1527, however, there was very little in the way of an extended theological defense of such a position in the initial years of the movement.

But as Baptist writers eventually took to defending their position, they did so largely on the grounds which we have laid out in previous chapters: namely, that the New Testament is silent on the practice of baptizing infants; that the biblical examples seem to presuppose the existence of faith in the recipients of baptism; that the New Testament church, in opposition to Old Testament Israel, is comprised only of those who are true believers and have been baptized (thus, excluding their young children); and that the sign of baptism is very different from circumcision in its intended administration, as the latter was primarily a national or racial sign which lacked the spiritual significance that attaches to baptism.

So how were such arguments received in their day? We have already noted the vehemence with which the mainstream Reformers opposed the Anabaptists and their distinctive theological emphases, but that fact serves to raise an important question: did the Reformers overreact to the appearance of the Anabaptists, who, after all, could have been valuable allies in the effort to overthrow Roman Catholicism in sixteenth century Europe? Or did they see something far more ominous in the theology of Anabaptism than just a good-spirited difference of opinion regarding the proper subjects of baptism amongst those who were otherwise like-minded?

While it must be noted that at least some of the persecution directed against the Anabaptists was in reaction to the activities and beliefs of a few of its more fanatical and infamous adherents, it is also true that in the Anabaptists' argument against infant baptism the Reformers saw a fundamental rejection of the Reformation itself. Indeed, so serious were these differences to Zwingli, the first-generation Swiss Reformer, that he could

---

[2] *Confessions and Catechisms of the Reformation*, ed. Mark A. Noll (Grand Rapids: Baker, 1995), 51-52.

characterize the controversy with Rome as "mere child's play" when compared to that with the Anabaptists.[3]

As far as the Reformers were concerned, the problem with believer's baptism (aside from its lack of scriptural support) is that it conflicts with the two governing principles which most closely capture the essence of Reformation theology: its God-centeredness and its covenant-centeredness. The first of these may be said to be the supreme underlying principle, but it is correct to say that the two of them represent the twin pillars upon which Reformed theology stands.

Infant Baptism is God-Centered

The most fundamental and profound distinction between the two sides in the debate over infant baptism is not the connection between faith and baptism, nor the significance of what takes place at its administration, but whether one views baptism primarily as a divine action of the Lord or as the work of human obedience.[4] This is the fixed point from which all of the other arguments flow.

In contrast to the Baptist position, which views baptism primarily as the willful act of the person baptized, and conditions its reception on the prior faith of the human recipient, the Reformed doctrine of baptism views the rite as one in which God is the principal actor. God is active in placing His sign and seal upon those whom He chooses, and just as with His decree of election to salvation, it is His sovereign good pleasure which determines those to whom it is to be administered.

Pierre Marcel points out that the verbs used in the baptismal texts of the New Testament are entirely passive in form. Thus, one *is baptized* or *receives* baptism, just as one receives circumcision.[5] Even the command to "repent and *be baptized*" implies a certain passivity on the part of the one undergoing baptism, for no one

---

[3] Schaff, 8.71.

[4] Edmund Schlink, *The Doctrine of Baptism*, trans. Herbert J.A. Bouman (St. Louis: Concordia Publishing, 1972), 169.

[5] Pierre Ch. Marcel, *The Biblical Doctrine of Infant Baptism*, trans. Philip Edgcumbe Hughes (New York: Westminster, 2000), 161.

ever self-administers the rite. Rather, even the adult believer merely *submits* himself to baptism, just as Jesus submitted Himself to the baptism of John. In baptism, it is Christ who is operative, "while the person baptized is the passive object of His deed."[6] In the Reformed understanding, then, the person coming for baptism does not so much perform an action as allow himself to be acted upon. And it should be obvious that the baptism of the infant children of believers accords perfectly with such an understanding of the nature of the sacrament.

B.B. Warfield commented upon this fact as follows:

> Every time we baptize an infant we bear witness that salvation is from God, that we cannot do any good thing to secure it, that we receive it from his hands as a sheer gift of his grace, and that we all enter the kingdom of heaven therefore as little children, who do not do, but are done for.[7]

Presenting our infant children for baptism is an acknowledgement that we (and they) are completely dependentupon the grace of God for all of our blessings. Indeed, because by means of infant baptism the child is received into the kingdom of God without any contribution of his own, there is no other act by which the church "confesses so unmistakably that it is God alone who saves man."[8]

In baptism we come to the Lord empty-handed, not to testify to our own faith before men, but in humble recognition that even the faith we possess is a gift of God's grace toward us. We acknowledge the same thing when we present our children for baptism, and with the same empty hands cling to the gracious promise of God that our little ones belong to Him as well.

As something which God undertakes to do, baptism is fundamentally a supernatural activity. It is God who impresses that person with His seal of ownership and ushers him or her into the kingdom, with all of the spiritual benefits and protection that

---

[6] Cullman, 15.

[7] Warfield, 1:329.

[8] Schlink, 160.

it offers. Thus, every time we baptize a person (child or adult) "a new victory is won over the hostile powers, as a new member is set at the place where he can be delivered from these powers."[9]

In the baptism of an infant child the church assumes a grave responsibility for that child's future spiritual nurture. And this obligation on the part of the church benefits the child from the very inception of physical life until its cessation. This idea is expressed beautifully by Marcel:

> If the Church pays attention to the demands of the administration of the covenant and considers those who have been born in it as being primarily entrusted to her care, if she knows how to avail herself of the theology of the covenant and of the psychological and pedagogical weapons which it affords, if she believes in God's promises and in His faithfulness, then she ought to reconsider her hasty judgments, too often formed without charity and with an altogether Pharisaic brutality – and which undoubtedly control her methods of work – against Protestants who are called "detached" or who have become "indifferent." She must learn once more to regard them lovingly as members of the covenant and of the people of God. She has an urgent and special ministry in respect of them, founded on the commands and promises of God ... She ought ceaselessly and in a thousand different ways to remind them of her existence, right up to the day when they are carried to the cemetery, without ever acknowledging herself defeated or resigning herself to the loss of such persons.[10]

Furthermore, baptism is a means of grace, not only for the recipient, but for the entire church as well. By means of baptism the faith of those who are privileged to witness the act is strengthened as the promise of God is displayed visually before their very eyes, and they are encouraged to "improve" upon their

---

[9] Cullman, 32.
[10] Marcel, 133-35.

own baptism. The parents of those who present their children for baptism are encouraged to serve God more faithfully when they reflect on the fact that God cares for the children that He has in grace given to them. And in all of this, God is glorified and His name is exalted amongst His people, who recognize Him as the giver of all that is good and blessed.[11]

In testifying to our complete dependence upon God for all things, as well as to the supernatural and corporate character of the sacraments, the practice of infant baptism is thoroughly God-centered. And it is because of this fact that the practice is an indispensable component of the system of Reformed theology, which views God, and not man, as the center of all things.

Infant Baptism is Covenant-Centered

In addition to being God-centered, infant baptism is also covenant-centered. By this we mean that the practice is rooted in, takes its significance from, and flows naturally out of, the covenant promises of God, most specifically displayed in His promise to be a God to believers and to their children. This is why the Reformed practice is sometimes referred to as "covenantal infant baptism," in order to distinguish it from those theologies of infant baptism that are not explicitly based upon the promises contained in the covenant of grace. The term appropriately stresses the fact that only those children who are born within the sphere of the covenant are entitled to receive the waters of baptism.

In view of the fact that we have already spent two full chapters propounding the covenantal basis for infant baptism, we will not devote any more time to covering that ground again. But what is important to note here is that it was the Reformers' rediscovery of the centrality of the covenant in God's plan of redemption that placed infant baptism back on its scriptural foundation. With the covenant of grace now recognized as the central organizing principle of the Bible's witness to that plan, Reformed theology quickly became *covenant theology*. And because covenant theology emphasizes the continuity of the promises and the people of

---

[11] Ibid., 228-29.

God, infant baptism once again assumed its rightful place as a sacrament of the covenant of grace.

On the other end of the spectrum are those who deny the unity of the covenant of grace, and see both the promises and the people of God as being broken up by the events of redemptive history, most especially by the life and death of Jesus Christ. As we noted back in chapter three, those who hold most consistently to this method of interpretation are known as dispensationalists. But the general impression of the discontinuity of Scripture is a common one, and finds expression in the beliefs and statements of many who would not formally fall into that theological category. As we also mentioned in that earlier chapter, not all Baptists are dispensationalists. But I am not aware of any individual person or church which adheres to the dispensational system of theology and does not also reject infant baptism.

Amongst those who deny the validity of infant baptism it is not uncommon to find a tendency to devalue anything associated with the Old Testament era, including its people. Circumcision is often seen as a purely carnal sign, given to a carnal people, while baptism is viewed as a spiritual and higher sign, given to a spiritual people. Some mistakenly associate the sign of circumcision with the Old Testament ceremonial law, and assign to it an exclusively national or racial significance. But those who do so seem to be forgetting that the sign of circumcision was given to Abraham hundreds of years before the ceremonial law was given to Moses.

The effect of this attitude toward Scripture and toward the essential unity of the covenants over time has led to what Marcel calls "a kind of Old Testament anti-semitism."[12] Calvin addressed such thoughts in his *Institutes*, where he wrote of those who interpret Scripture in this way as follows:

> In asserting a difference of covenant they corrupt and destroy Scripture with rough audacity. They depict the Jews as a carnal and brutish people who had no other covenant with God than one concerning only this temporal life, and

---

[12] Ibid., 81.

no other promise than one offering merely present and corruptible benefits. If such was the case what remains to us other than to regard this nation as a herd of swine whom our Lord wished to nourish in their sty for a while in order to let them perish eternally?[13]

Calvin's words here may seem like an unduly harsh judgment upon those who do not share his covenantal convictions, but they serve to illustrate well the point that we are trying to make – that rejection of the covenantal view of Scripture goes hand-in-hand with a rejection of Reformed theology in general, and of infant baptism in particular. We would also note that the same domino effect tends to play itself out when the order of events is reversed; that is, those who call themselves Reformed but later reject infant baptism will often come to subsequently reject Reformed theology altogether.

It is for this reason, as I stated at the beginning of the book, that I no longer believe that the use of the term *Reformed Baptist* is legitimate if we wish to speak with any sort of theological precision. Too many Christians have come to think that being *Reformed* means simply adhering to the doctrines of grace, otherwise known as the Five Points of Calvinism. But the Reformed faith is much richer and more inclusive of scriptural truth than that. As central as the Five Points are to the system of Reformed theology, it is unfair to reduce it to that one area of concern. After all, it was Calvin himself who taught that there were three marks of a true church, one of which was the proper administration of the sacraments. Clearly, he did not make allowance for any such term as *Reformed Baptist* in his theological lexicon.

Professor David Engelsma states the matter in this way:

In rejecting the doctrine of the one covenant of grace, basic to which is the inclusion of the children of believers in the covenant and their baptism as infants, all Baptists part company with the Reformed faith. Pastor

---

[13] Ibid., (quoting from Calvin's *Institutes*, 4.16.10).

Oosterman finds this judgment objectionable, inasmuch as some Baptists today call themselves Reformed. They suppose that they have a right to this glorious name, because they confess, more or less soundly, the 'Five Points of Calvinism.'

But is it lawful for Baptists to claim the name *Reformed* when they reject a doctrine and corresponding practice that both the Reformed tradition and the Reformed creeds designate as essential to the Reformed faith? May a church then also deny, for example, the doctrine of sovereign, eternal predestination and yet claim to be Reformed on the ground that it does maintain other doctrines that are taught in the Reformed tradition and confessed in the Reformed creeds? May I similarly reject the teaching so precious to Baptists, namely 'believer's baptism,' but still present myself to the world as a Baptist?[14]

Because baptism is a holy "sign and seal of the covenant of grace" (WCF 28:1), and one of the means of grace whereby God strengthens and nourishes biblical faith, it is inextricably bound up with our understanding of the gospel. After all, the covenant of grace is a covenant of election. That explains why it is so difficult for someone to dispense with the Reformed understanding of the sacrament and not have it eventually influence their understanding of the gospel as well. What distinguishes the Reformed (i.e., biblical) gospel from all other imitations is its unwavering insistence that biblical faith is the product of "God's free and special grace alone" (WCF 10:2). But when one begins to view baptism in rationalistic terms, ignoring its supernatural and corporate character, and assigning to it the status of "the badge of a Christian man's profession," it is all too easy to begin viewing biblical faith in the same way. The history of the Protestant church in America, as our discussion below will demonstrate, provides ample evidence for such an assertion.

---

[14] Engelsma, 50-51.

So How Did We Get Here?

At this point, a question arises naturally from all that has been written up to now: if infant baptism was indeed the practice of the early church, and was the near universal doctrine of the Reformed church as well, how is it that we have gotten to the place where the vast majority of evangelical (Bible-believing) churches in America adhere only to the practice of believer's baptism?

A proper answer to that question demands more space than we have luxury to give it here. But suffice it to say that the distinctively American brand of evangelicalism which arose out of the first and second Great Awakenings, and the frontier missionary efforts of the eighteenth and nineteenth centuries, in many ways bore little resemblance to the form of Christianity which had been planted here by the European settlers of the prior century.

The "rugged individualism" of the American frontier tended to shun all expressions of religious authority, whether of the human or written variety. This meant that received traditions were looked on with suspicion (or even contempt), and the private and personal interpretation of the Scriptures was exalted as superior to reliance on the collective wisdom of those who had come before. The phrase "No creed but the Bible" represented the popular sentiment of the day. Alexander Campbell, one of the early leaders of the second Great Awakening, arrogantly proclaimed that he had "endeavored to read the scriptures as though no one had read them before me."[15]

New denominations sprang up overnight, although there was just as much tendency to shun denominational affiliations and structures altogether. To be sure, not all of these individuals and groups opposed the practice of infant baptism. And some of them were not even Christian. But these disparate groups all shared one common purpose. Although they did not necessarily coordinate their efforts in any official capacity, as Nathan Hatch tells it, they were united in that together they

---

[15] Nathan O. Hatch, *The Democratization of American Christianity* (New Haven, CT: Yale University Press, 1989), 179.

"launched a ferocious crusade against *every facet* of Calvinist orthodoxy" [emphasis added].[16]

Moreover, this unraveling of the received Protestant tradition was not confined only to the frontier and the new denominations taking root there. Lewis Bevens Schenck, in his fascinating book on the subject, chronicles how the influence of the first Great Awakening loosened the commitment to infant baptism even amongst the Presbyterian churches of New England in the eighteenth century. As the revivalist emphasis upon conscious conversion only after undergoing an intense emotional struggle was exalted as the normative Christian experience, uncertainty as to the status of children in the covenant became common, which eventually led to a laxity in administering the sacrament to the children of believers.[17] Schenck describes the disastrous (and truly sad) consequences of this development as follows:

> The principle of the Reformed faith, that the child brought up under Christian influence should never know a time when love to God was not an active principle in its life, was displaced by an assumption that even the offspring of the godly were born enemies of God and must await the crisis of conversion … Instead of growing up with the spirit and character of members of Christ's family, appreciating their privileges and feeling their responsibilities, they were supposed to grow up with the spirit and character of the world. The children of the church, with the seal of God's covenant on their foreheads, were practically cast out, to be classed and thence to class themselves in form and feeling with the ungodly and profane …[18]

The new movement was anti-intellectual, anti-clerical, and doggedly individualistic. In this environment, Baptists of all stripes flourished. Their emphasis upon decisional evangelism,

---

[16] Hatch, 170.
[17] Schenck, 1, 81.
[18] Ibid., 153-54.

the methods employed in carrying out those efforts, and the congregational structure of church government that they propounded, all tended to appeal to the emerging culture. When the influence of dispensationalism, which was developed in England in the first half of the nineteenth century and took serious root in conservative churches in America in the twentieth, is added in to the mix, it becomes easy to see how and why we got to the place where Reformed infant baptism has been all but snuffed out in our day.

What we are left with is an American Christianity that has imbibed much of the individualistic culture that developed during that time period. These cultural influences are reflected in any number of different aspects of the modern church, from the evangelistic methods used, to the loss of the corporate sense of baptism, to the multiplication of non-denominational churches, and especially in the fact that church membership is shunned by hordes of individual Christians who have decided that they are under no obligation whatsoever to bind themselves in covenant with the visible Body of Christ, or to place themselves under the oversight and authority of those who have been charged with shepherding them. Whereas many of the Jews in Jesus' day were guilty of relying *exclusively* upon their corporate identity as physical descendants of Abraham, and thus members of the nation of Israel, we in the modern American church are guilty of the opposite tendency: viewing ourselves almost exclusively from the standpoint of our personal individualism.[19] And with such a philosophical framework undergirding our biblical interpretation, it is no wonder that the household baptismal passages in Acts do not seem to make an impression upon us.

Though it may sound contradictory at first, I am no longer surprised by the lack of support for infant baptism that I encounter today, but I never cease to be amazed by it. It no longer surprises me because of all the reasons we have laid out above. But it amazes me that so many Christians today are not just unaware of the arguments for the practice, but so often appear

---

[19] Johnson, 8-9.

to be *indifferent* to hearing them. Although they may not express it verbally, many of them seem to have implicitly accepted the argument that infant baptism is merely a holdover from medieval Catholicism, something the Reformers felt constrained to retain lest the church fall into complete chaos.

Even in churches where it is officially affirmed and practiced, it is not uncommon to find individual members who view the baptism of their infant children as optional or ultimately unimportant. This too no longer surprises me, however, since so many of those in Reformed churches have come into them from the broader evangelical world, after becoming convinced of the truthfulness of the doctrines of grace.

But the Reformers of the sixteenth century considered the practice as anything but optional or unimportant. And far from it being the vestige of an "incomplete Reformation," the Reformed doctrine of infant baptism bore no theological resemblance to Roman Catholic baptism whatsoever. So different was the conception of Reformed baptism from that of the Roman Catholic that the Scottish Reformer John Knox could say that the latter had become so adulterated that "whosoever offers their children to the papistical baptism, offers them to the devil."[20]

Knox's comments demonstrate that it is high time to abandon the insulting notion that the Reformers did not have the courage to dispense with infant baptism, even though they may have believed it to be without basis in Scripture. The truth is that *nothing* escaped the Reformers' biblical scrutiny as they set out to purge the church of its superstitious and unbiblical elements. They had no problem completely redefining the meaning of the other biblical sacrament, the Lord's Supper, despite the popular veneration of the "host" by the medieval faithful, and reducing the number of sacraments from seven to two. Rest assured that if they had believed that infant baptism was not the biblical practice, they would have thrown it on the trash heap!

---

[20] John Knox, *Answers to Some Questions Concerning Baptism, etc. (1556).* Accessed September 5, 2001. Online: http://www.swrb.com/newlett/actualNLs/answersq.htm.

One need only briefly peruse the writings of men like Luther, Calvin, and Knox in order to see how passionate they were about the practice of baptizing the children of the covenant. The same men who fought for the principle of *Sola Scriptura* ("Scripture Alone"), over against a medieval church that placed tradition on an equal footing with Holy Writ, knew their Bibles better than any who had come before them for more than a thousand years. They recognized a biblical practice when they saw one, and for them the topic was no side issue. They saw infant baptism for what it was – a God-centered practice which flowed naturally from the covenantal structure of the Bible. In short, they saw it as an *indispensable* component of Reformed theology.

Chapter 9

The Importance of the Matter

When we survey the religious landscape of twenty-first century America, and the state of the Christian church in particular, we cannot help but be struck by the incredible diversity that we see exhibited. The sheer number of different religions and individual Christian denominations around us is staggering, and seems to increase more with each passing year. Although Christianity remains the dominant religious affiliation by far, the true church today finds itself in the midst of an increasingly hostile audience. A large percentage of those claiming to be Christian do not attend church services of any kind on a regular basis, and the claims of Christianity to be the exclusive reservoir of the truth are dismissed, and even derided, by many who come from within the confines of the visible church itself.

Nevertheless, within this diverse religious environment there exists a core group of those whom God has chosen to believe on His Son, Jesus Christ, and cling to the truth of His word. They come from many different denominations and backgrounds, but they have one thing in common – the blood of Christ has cleansed them from their sins once and for all. And they share a common vision as well – to proclaim the good news about Christ's death and to see the nations come to that same knowledge.

Obviously, Reformed Christians and Baptist Christians are united to one another through the blood of Christ, despite their differences on the subject of baptism. There is one body of Christ, and the denominational distinctions that men choose to make do not change that reality one bit. Thankfully, both sides recognize that the issue of baptism does not determine our standing with Jesus Christ, or jeopardize our relationship of trust in Him. Good Christians can, and do, disagree on this fundamental matter of the faith.

Given this reality, and the desire for Bible-believing Christians of whatever stripe to be co-belligerents in the fight against the moral and cultural degradation that is taking place in Western society today, a thoughtful Christian could legitimately ask if dividing ourselves over the issue of baptism is really a good idea any longer. In the increasingly hostile environment that Christians find themselves today, it might be asked if our denominational divisions have finally outlived their usefulness. More to the point, is the doctrine of baptism really that important?

These are good questions, and it will not do to dismiss them with pat answers that do not also speak to the more fundamental underlying issue – whether it is an inherent weakness of the Protestant Church that it is splintered into so many different denominations. We'll seek to answer this latter question first and then address whether or not baptism as a specific point of contention is important enough to divide over.

In answering the question of whether or not it is a weakness of the Protestant Church that it is so splintered, we are really forced to look at it from two different angles. In the first instance, if we mean to say that it is a shame (and thus, a weakness in that sense) that the Protestant Church is not united into one single, large body of faithful believers, so that our resources are used most effectively for the proclamation of the gospel, and to fight against those who seek to destroy Christ's church, then I wholeheartedly agree with the statement. In fact, it is hard to imagine anyone taking issue with it in that sense.

One of the greatest lost opportunities of all time occurred in 1529 at the Colloquy of Marburg, when Martin Luther and Ulrich Zwingli were unable to reach agreement on a single declaration out of fifteen which were under discussion, that of the meaning of the Lord's Supper. Had the two sides been able to find agreement on that issue and joined forces, the religious landscape of sixteenth century Europe might just have assumed a very different character than it eventually did, with the national (and then even smaller) divisions which in time arose and kept the new movement fragmented in fighting against a common enemy – the Church of Rome.

But if the question is posed so as to imply that it is a weakness in the sense that it demonstrates the problem of leaving the Bible to be interpreted without the final authority of a self-appointed magisterium, then I would take very serious issue with such a statement. For I believe that, far from being a weakness of the church, it is actually one of its greatest *strengths*. The Protestant church of the sixteenth century took a stand for the truth, and that stand cost it tens of thousands of lives. But in the process it established the principle that the Bible was for all men, and not just an enlightened few who were unaccountable to no one.

It may indeed be a shame that the Protestant church then very quickly divided over a number of issues (not just baptism), and remains so until this day, but it is because of its commitment to the truth of Scripture that such divisions arose. Just as we might wish that Luther and Zwingli had come to an agreement in 1529, we may at least take comfort in the fact that the truth of Scripture was important enough to separate over, and even die for.

All of which is not to say that every little theological squabble which has caused denominations to splinter over the centuries has been of sufficient importance to have led to such serious consequences. But it is a strength, not a weakness, of the Protestant church that God's truth has always been the ultimate standard for confession and ecclesiastical fellowship.

In our modern culture, where truth has become relative, the common refrain amongst many postmodernists is to forget about our differences and focus on what unites us. We might all agree that there are certain essentials around which we can gather and continue to call one another brothers and sisters in Christ. But we must be careful to not consign certain doctrines, such as infant baptism, to the category of inconsequential, or say that it is a matter of indifference as to whether it is practiced according to the Bible's injunctions.

In his book *Christianity and Liberalism*, J. Gresham Machen wrote about the modern church's drift toward liberalism, and the tendency that brings to not only minimize theological differences, but to avoid doctrinal discussions altogether. Machen wrote in 1923, and the situation that he described has only gotten worse since then. In the book, he contrasts the modern church's doctrinal indifference with the understanding that prevailed during the Reformation period – that doctrine was not merely important, but (at least in some cases) worth dying for. In commenting upon the split between Luther and Zwingli, Machen wrote as follows:

> It was a great calamity indeed. But the calamity was due to the fact Luther (as we believe) was wrong about the Lord's Supper; and it would have been a far greater calamity if being wrong about the Supper he had represented the whole question as a trifling affair … A Luther who would have compromised with regard to the Lord's Supper never would have said at the Diet of Worms, 'Here I stand, I cannot do otherwise, God help me, Amen.' Indifferentism about doctrine makes no heroes of the faith.[1]

As Machen reminds us, truth in spiritual matters is important, and fighting for it will not always make one popular. In Christian

---

[1] J. Gresham Machen, *Christianity and Liberalism* (Grand Rapids: Eerdmans, 1994), 50-51.

charity and love, we can and should continue to seek reunion and common dialogue with other Bible-believing churches, and never give up hope that one day God's church will be far less splintered than it is today. But we must also be careful not to do so at the expense of His truth, for a church which finds unity only in dispensing with anything that causes divisions is not likely to stand against the cold winds of opposition that are only becoming stronger around us every day.

But what about the more specific question we have posed here – is the doctrine of infant baptism really so important as to divide over, if necessary? To some extent we have already answered this question in the last couple of chapters, where we looked at the implications that attend abandoning infant baptism and embracing the believer's baptism model. But I am convinced that a direct appeal to Scripture should serve to settle the matter of the importance of infant baptism once and for all. To that end, we will appeal to two separate passages, one from the Old Testament and one from the New Testament.

The Old Testament passage is found in the fourth chapter of Exodus, where we read how God called upon Moses to return to Egypt for the purpose of delivering His people from bondage, so that they might serve Him in the land that He had promised them. Then, in verses 24-26 we read these surprising words:

> And it came to pass on the way, at the encampment, that the Lord met him and sought to kill him. Then Zipporah took a sharp stone and cut off the foreskin of her son and cast it at Moses' feet, and said, 'Surely you are a husband of blood to me!' So He let him go. Then she said, 'You are a husband of blood!' – because of the circumcision.

This has to be one of the most incredible passages in all of Scripture. Here is Moses, on his way to Egypt to bring the Israelites out of bondage at God's express command, being confronted by God, who is there to take his life and put an end to the venture altogether! And what great offense had Moses committed to bring such an end upon himself and the hopes of all Israel? He had failed to circumcise his son. It was only the quick action of Moses' wife, Zipporah, which caused the Lord to relent and spare his life.

It is hard to imagine how God could have given a more profound testimony to the importance which He attaches to administering the covenant sign to our children. While some have tried to minimize the force of this passage by arguing that it was only of such importance in this instance because Moses was the mediator of the old covenant, my response to that is, "How much *less* have I the right to expect that God would bear with me in such disobedience?" If God was prepared to dispose of one so integral to the future plans for His covenant people, on what basis would I plead for leniency if guilty of the same sin? Let's face it – we all have gifts which we can use for the benefit of Christ's church, but (thankfully) the loss of any single one of us will not cause the whole structure to collapse. May the same thing be said with respect to Moses, however?

When we come to the New Testament, we are told that Jesus rebuked the Pharisees and lawyers who refused to be baptized by John and thereby "rejected the will of God for themselves" (Luke 7:30). Though the issue here is John's baptism, not the one which Christ later commanded in His name, that fact merely causes us to raise the same sort of question that we did above: if John's baptism was that important, how much more, then, should we expect that neglecting Christian baptism is likewise a rejection of the will of God, and thus worthy of Christ's rebuke?

The Westminster Confession of Faith (28:5) declares that it is "a great sin to contemn or neglect" the ordinance of baptism. Given all of the evidence from Scripture that has been documented here, it is difficult to escape the conclusion that the refusal of Christian parents to baptize their covenant children constitutes such neglect, and renders them guilty of the great sin of which the Confession speaks.

We may give thanks for the fact that in this age of greater grace God has apparently chosen not to exercise His prerogative to take the lives of those who are guilty of this sin; but neither must we lose sight of the fact that the God who sought to take Moses' life over such a deficiency is the same God whom we worship today. And so His gracious forbearance in this matter may never be used as an excuse to sin. Of course, no true Christian ever wants to be in the position of opposing God's will. Thus, the leaders of Christ's church bear a great responsibility for seeing to it that they do not aid those under their care to do just that.

In seeking to deal with the issues we have raised here, every Christian parent who is considering withholding the sacrament of baptism from their young children must ultimately ask himself or herself these questions:

- Do I want to be in the position of holding that, in this age of the fullness of grace in Christ, the children of Christian parents are in an *inferior* position to those under the prior dispensation, who were entitled to receive the sign and seal of the covenant of grace to which their parents were already parties?

- Do I want to be in the position of disregarding Jesus' injunction to let the little children come to Him and instead to exclude them as outsiders and strangers to the covenants of promise?

- Do I want to be in the position of potentially casting public doubt upon God's promise to be a God to believers *and their children* by withholding baptism from my covenant child?

- Do I want to be in the position of limiting the significance of baptism to the 'badge of a Christian man's profession' and thereby minimize or altogether ignore the supernatural character of the rite as an action in which God Himself is involved?

- Do I want to deprive my child of the opportunity of improving upon his or her baptism during the early years of their life as they witness those coming after them receiving the sign?

- Do I really want to effectively treat my child as a 'little heathen' when Christ has said that "of such is the kingdom of God"?

- Do I really want to deprive my child of the blessing of God's covenant sign in spite of all the Bible's warnings that to do so will result in that child's being "cut-off" from God's people?

- And finally, do I really want to say that withholding the covenant sign from my child is not a serious offense to God when He has clearly shown otherwise in His Word?

As we conclude our study, let me say that I am sensitive to the argument that, given the non-essential nature of the doctrine of baptism, as well as the fact that the biblical data is not as explicit as we might like at this point, we should in Christian charity and humility acknowledge our own possibility for error in this matter, and thus act accordingly toward our Christian brothers and sisters who may not see things the same way as us on this issue. It is a fact that many Christians today wince when they read the writings of the great Reformers of the sixteenth and seventeenth centuries. They see the rhetorical combativeness of men like Luther and Calvin as divisive and even counterproductive in our modern cultural context. Thus, we are urged to adopt a less polemical stance, and make allowance for our differences without imputing the worst of motives to those who may disagree with us.

I will acknowledge that there is a great deal of wisdom in such cautionary pleas. It can hardly be disputed that Christians are called by God to be charitable and humble toward one another, even when we find ourselves disagreeing over certain matters. But at the same time we must recognize that our doctrine of baptism is bound up with our understanding of the gospel, and that the position we take on this issue has the potential to influence the way in which we view the grace of God in salvation. Our doctrine of baptism may not ultimately determine our relationship with Christ, but neither is it a merely peripheral matter, or one of no great importance. As

Machen reminds us, indifference to doctrine makes no heroes of the faith; and in an age when truth has become relative, and there is little, if anything, which is considered worth fighting (much less dying) for, the modern Christian church is sorely in need of heroes.

Hence, we must be guided by a desire to achieve the proper balance in our debate here – one which recognizes our unity in the Spirit and extends to all Christians certain common courtesies, but does not gloss over our differences as if they were of no import, or (worse yet) adopt the postmodern notion that the truth of this matter is itself a relative proposition. Important matters of God's revealed truth are always worth earnestly contending for (Jude 3), even when it involves contending with our fellow Christians. Individual believers may fall into the trap of treating the issue as negotiable, but if God cares for the sparrow that falls from the tree, you can be certain that He cares a great deal more about whether or not your child (His child!) receives the covenant sign to which he or she is entitled.

Having thus pleaded my case for the importance of this debate, however, let me finish on this note: as important as I feel this issue is for the life of the church and its people, I would sooner enjoy a fellowship meal or join hands in a common cause with a thousand Baptists who love the Lord Jesus Christ, than with one single unbeliever who faithfully practices infant baptism. I might disagree with my Baptist brother's refusal to administer the covenant sign to his children. I might even agree with the Westminster Confession that in so doing, he is guilty of a great sin. But the blood of Christ that saves us is also sufficient to cover our ongoing sins of judgment, including this one. We may separate over this issue into distinct theological traditions, but we are ultimately united in the invisible body of Christ, which is the true church.

And so it is my earnest prayer that the Lord would use this brief attempt at theological persuasion – yes, to bring some around to the position which has been set forth here – but for the larger purposes of insuring that our covenant children receive the sign to which they are entitled, and for bringing us all closer to the unity which only the Spirit can provide. May the Lord unify His Church that we might go forward together, proclaiming the name of Jesus Christ to those yet in darkness, "till we all come to the unity of the faith and of the knowledge of the Son of God" (Eph. 4:13).

The Sixty Second Case for Infant Baptism

• God made an everlasting covenant with Abraham and commanded him to circumcise every male child in his household, which was to serve as a sign of the covenant between them (Gen. 17:9-14)

• This covenant, which was a covenant of election, finds its fulfillment in the promised seed, Jesus Christ, and continues in force until all those for whom He died are welcomed into His kingdom (Gal. 3:16–4:7; Heb. 6:13-18; 9:15; 1 John 2:25)

• With the death and resurrection of Christ, the sign of the covenant was changed to baptism, in order to reflect the reality that a bloody sign (circumcision) was no longer appropriate, now that Christ had shed His blood for the remission of sins (Heb. 9:23–10:14; Matt. 28:19-20)

• The New Testament is devoid of any language suggesting that the rules for membership in the church have changed from what had prevailed for two thousand years. On the contrary, because the new covenant era is an era of greater grace, the application of the covenant sign is no longer limited only to males, but now encompasses all the children of believers (Acts 2:38-39)

• Because baptism has replaced circumcision as the sign of the covenant, Paul connected the significance of the two rites, and described baptism as the 'circumcision of Christ' (Col. 2:11-12)

• The household baptismal accounts in Acts demonstrate that the principle of family solidarity that applied in the Old Testament period still holds true in the New Testament era. They also make it highly probable that Acts, contrary to popular opinion, contains explicit accounts of children being baptized (Acts 10:24-48; 16:11-15; 16:25-34)

• Paul declared that the children of Christian parents were 'holy' (1 Cor. 7:14)

• Jesus rebuked His disciples for trying to prevent believers from bringing their infant children to Him in order to receive His blessing. He told them that "of such is the kingdom of God," and warned that those who reject the reception of little children in His name thereby reject *Him* (Mark 10:13-16; Matt. 18:1-6)